Serving *All* Urban Consumers

Serving *All* Urban Consumers

A marketing approach to water services in low and middle-income countries

Book 1: Guidance for governments' enabling role

Kevin Sansom, Sam Kayaga, Richard Franceys,
Cyrus Njiru, Sue Coates and Srinivas Chary

Water, Engineering and Development Centre
Loughborough University
2004

Water, Engineering and Development Centre,
Loughborough University,
Leicestershire, LE11 3TU, UK

Institute of Water and Environment
Cranfield University
Silsoe, Bedford
MK45 4DT UK

Produced as part of a WEDC/IWE partnership

© Water, Engineering and Development Centre; 2004

ISBN 13 Paperback: 978 1 84380 054 5
ISBN Ebook: 9781788533508
Book DOI: http://dx.doi.org/10.3362/9781788533508

A catalogue record for this book is available from the British Library.

A reference copy of this publication is also available online at:
http://www.lboro.ac.uk/wedc/publications/sftup.htm

Sansom, K., Kayaga. S., Franceys, R., Njiru, C., Coates, S. and Chary, S. (2004) Serving all urban consumers - A marketing approach to water services in low and middle-income countries. Book 1: Guidance for government's enabling role. WEDC, Loughborough University, UK.

WEDC (The Water, Engineering and Development Centre) at Loughborough University in the UK is one of the world's leading institutions concerned with education, training, research and consultancy for the planning, provision and management of physical infrastructure for development in low- and middleincome countries.

This edition is reprinted and distributed by Practical Action Publishing.
Since 1974, Practical Action Publishing has published and disseminated books and information in support of international development work throughout the world. Practical Action Publishing trades only in support of its parent charity objectives and any profits are covenanted back to Practical Action (Charity Reg. No. 247257, Group VAT Registration No. 880 9924 76).

This document is an output from a project funded by the UK
Department for International Development (DFID)
for the benefit of low-income countries.
The views expressed are not necessarily those of DFID.

Acknowledgements

The financial support of the Department for International Development of the British Government is gratefully acknowledged. The valuable assistance and contributions of engineers, managers and consultants in our field research cities is much appreciated by the authors. Key people include: A. Narender in Guntor, India, G. Bhattarai in various small towns in Nepal, S .K . Gup ta, Agra, India and Ms A. Kamalie for the Lesotho report. Many other utility, NGO and college staff provided valuable assistance in our fieldwork in the main research locations: Mombasa, Kampala, Durban and Guntor for which we are most grateful.

The advice and review work of Dennis Mwanza, Alison Wedgwood, Kimberly Clarke and Guy Howard is also appreciated.

List of boxes

List of figures

List of tables

Contents

Chapter 1

Overview

1.1   Introduction and document overview

Managing water services and sanitation successfully is like any other business, where the responsible organization seeks to: keep customers satisfied, increase market share, and maximize revenues. This entails using commercial and market orientated approaches, which have been successfully utilised by utilities throughout the world and are increasingly being used in developing countries.

A key question to consider is how best commercial approaches to utility management can be adapted to serving low income areas so that sustainable services are achieved? There are many instances of this being done successfully and this issue is addressed in this series of three books entitled: *'Serving All Urban Consumers'*. This title is intended to be a challenge to network utilities and to the governments who help create their enabling environment.

The specific purpose of this series of books is to provide appropriate guidance on how water utilities working with other key stakeholders, can meet the needs and demands of urban water consumers - including the poor - through developing an understanding of the needs and demands of all consumer groups, and by the adaptation of a commercial/ marketing approach. These documents are suitable for public or private sector providers, who should be encouraged to pilot new approaches before eventual scaling up.

Book 1 (this publication) focuses on how governments can support an enabling environment, both for utilities and other stakeholders, to work effectively towards achieving these objectives. Unless governments and regulators do provide an appropriate enabling environment for the key stakeholders to serve the poor, then substantial improvements are unlikely to be achieved. A summary of the contents of Book 1 is as follows:

- Chapter 1 provides an overview of the experiences and challenges in the sector, as well as examples from around the world where innovative marketing-type approaches have been used successfully.

- Chapter 2 summarizes marketing approaches to water services for all consumer groups - that is described in more detail in Book 2 -guidance notes for managers. If the relevant government departments and regulators understand how marketing principles can best be adapted to the urban water sector, they can encourage utilities to utilise or adapt such approaches for serving low income areas.

1

- Chapter 3 considers how to improve incentives for different stakeholders in order to provide better services in low-income communities. Governments and regulators have substantial influence over the various incentives for utilities and civil society institutions to improve services.

- Chapter 4 considers how best governments and regulators can support utilities and other stakeholders in improving services to all consumer groups.

1.2   Who is this book for?

These summary guidance notes (Book 1) are intended for use by senior and middle-level managers in government departments and regulators who are developing an enabling environment for improving urban water services to all consumer groups including the poor. This book should also be of interest to sector advisors and senior utility managers.

This book is complemented by Book 2, which is targeted at managers and is a more comprehensive publication that examines how to use marketing approaches for urban water services to serve all consumers. Book 3 gives a detailed explanation of the PREPP methodology for utility consultation with low-income communities, including demand assessment and decision making about improved service levels.

Having undertaken detailed research based on strategic marketing plans in cities in Africa and India to prove the concepts, these three books are designed as simplified approaches that will give sufficient accuracy to be implemented immediately. The goal is for 'good enough' marketing and business plans that encourage early achievement of a universal service obligation.

We hope that the guidelines will also assist civil society organizations, whether water consumer organizations or CBOs and NGOs acting on behalf of the unserved poor, detailing what can reasonably be expected as good practice utility service in the sector and the potential roles of government.

1.3   Urban water context

Many governments in developing countries have adopted policies for providing better services for the urban poor, including water supply. This is in recognition of the experiences of low-income communities who are either unserved by water utilities or their municipalities, or they experience inadequate service levels and have to resort to other expensive or unprotected water sources. People living in informal settlements often pay high prices to water vendors or incur high coping costs in terms of time spent on collecting water. Only limited progress has been achieved in implementing these poverty reduction policies in the urban water sector.

How can urban water utilities provide better services for more of their expanding populations, including low-income communities, while improving the financial viability and credit worthiness of the utility? The people without adequate water supply and sanitation services often live in the unplanned, informal and illegal slums, the low-income settlements of the metropolitan and secondary cities. The task of filling this service gap is further compounded by the rapid growth of population in the urban areas of low-income countries.

Network water utilities are well placed to provide cheaper and more convenient piped water supplies compared with alternative providers such as vendors. The difficulties arise in planning, justifying and implementing service expansion in a sustainable manner. If the utilities, with their potential economies of scale, are able to capture a larger share of the 'water markets' in their cities and towns, at a fair price for each group of customers, they should be able to reduce the price that the poor currently have to pay for water and dramatically improve services, whilst ensuring the utilities' long-term financial viability.

The present situation is that utilities tend to price their water below cost, a subsidy which is then absorbed by the middle- and high-income groups who already have household water connections. The poor then have to pay more for a limited supply of poorer quality water, often delivered less conveniently by the vendors or other sources outside the utility's operations. However, capturing a larger share of the water market cannot be achieved by perpetuating the conventional 'one size fits all' approach. Traditionally utilities have offered consumers a conventional, full pressure, buried pipe household connection only if they live in 'legal' areas and pay a large connection fee. This approach automatically excludes about half the population in many cities.

1.4 Lessons for serving the poor

Water services providers and the governments who support and regulate them generally have two key objectives:

- To improve water services and increase service coverage, so that all consumers, including the poor, have adequate provision.

- To ensure utilities are financially sustainable - and therefore creditworthy - so that they can raise the funding to invest further.

To meet the needs of the poor whilst remaining financially viable water utilities have to learn to differentiate their services and prices of service provision. This entails offering and supporting a variety of viable service options (e.g. in-house or yard connections or water kiosks), as well as payment and management options to the various consumer groups. Only by this approach can they hope to meet the needs of their customers, present and potential where they are, not where the utility would like them to be. This approach means adopting and adapting the marketing techniques that the consumer goods and service industries have long had to use to ensure their commercial survival in a competitive market.

The value of partnerships is clear, particularly where utilities cannot provide services directly to certain areas for whatever reason and there is the potential to form partnerships as part of shared management arrangements with either small water enterprises such as vendors or with community-based organizations. In addition, in unserved areas that are far from pipe networks, a utility can provide information to potential customers about how to seek alternative water supply options such as borewells and rainwater harvesting, until the utility is able to serve those areas. By such means the utility is improving its reputation as a consumer-focused organization and developing trust amongst existing and potential customers.

There is evidence that utilities can do far more directly to serve the unplanned and often illegal low-income areas that have traditionally been ignored. In recent years a number of utilities have demonstrated that it is possible to differentiate service and prices to meet the needs of the poor. As part of the research that forms the basis for these guidance notes, and through complementary research, we have investigated those suppliers, public and private, that have been most successful at differentiating their services and prices to serve low-income customers, wherever they live. The examples described come from public utilities in South Africa and India as well as from private operators in Argentina, Bolivia and the Philippines.

The research also demonstrates, however, that services to low-income customers cannot be sustainable unless they are considered in the context of a long-term and city-wide strategy. It is not possible to give all customers exactly what they want at the price they want to pay. There has to be a balancing of different services and prices so that overall the utility achieves sufficient revenue to pay the costs of delivery to all consumers. In our desire to serve low-income consumers in the best possible way at the lowest price we also have to be aware of the overall impact on utility efficiency and sustainability.

Therefore we have also included in this document an introduction to the strategic marketing approach that is necessary to ensure overall viability of service to all consumers, the necessity for which is included in the title. Serving the lowest-income consumers also demands an efficient utility selling water to higher income customers at a cost-reflective price. Our international research partners have tested this methodology in six urban areas with varying degrees of detail: Kampala, Uganda (Kayaga); Mombasa, Kenya (Njiru); Lesotho (Kamalie); Guntur, India (Narender and Chary); Agra, India (Gupta; and various small towns in Nepal (Bhattarai).

A fully functioning and sustainable water utility is clearly the key to any attempt to better serve the poor (Water and Sanitation Programme, 2002). Poor utility performance hurts the poor more than others, as they are usually the first to be affected when service is rationed or there is low pressure; hence the need for a strategic approach.

The research results suggest that in most situations it is possible to develop a financially viable marketing plan that can enable a city to serve the needs of all consumers in partnership with other key stakeholders.

1.5 Water, sanitation and urban poverty reduction

There is overwhelming evidence of the health and economic benefits of improved water supply and sanitation for households and individuals. Table 1.1 highlights the key effects or adverse impacts of inadequate water supply and sanitation on poverty dimensions such as household income, health, education, and gender/social inclusion. Low-income communities who experience poor services are particularly prone to the adverse effects listed in the table.

Effective programmes that focus on water supply and sanitation services for the poor can make positive contributions to improving health and economic productivity in low-income countries, and are therefore a vital component of any effort to reduce poverty. Water utilities in partnerships with other key stakeholders have a vital role to play in the urban context.

Table 1.1. Linkages between water and sanitation and poverty[1]

Poverty dimensions	Inadequate water, sanitation and hygiene - Potential key effects
Income	High proportion of household budget used on obtaining water Reduced income earning potential because of: · Poor health · Increased time spent collecting water · Less opportunity for businesses requiring water inputs
Health	Increase in illnesses related to water and sanitation Stunting from diarrhoea caused by malnutrition Reduced life expectancy
Education	Reduced school attendance by children (especially girls) due to ill health, or lack of available sanitation or water collection points
Gender and social inclusion	Burdens borne disproportionately by women, limiting their entry into the cash economy

1. Source: Adapted from Bosch et al. (2001)

The percentage of poor people living on less than a US$1 per day in South Asia is 40 per cent and in Sub-Saharan Africa is 46 per cent (World Bank, 2000)Source: . Informal settlements and unplanned areas are generally growing faster than more middle and high-income areas, so governments and other stakeholders need to be innovative in their efforts to improve services and reduce poverty.

Over 75 per cent of the urban poor in Africa get their water from small-scale providers such as vendors, water tankers, etc. (Collignon and Vezina, 2000) and about half the people living in urban areas of Africa are not served by a piped water supply. The gap created by the low service coverage is often filled by small-scale independent water service providers, who generally charge prices that are many times greater than the piped water in the same city.

There are clear opportunities for utilities in cities to provide water service options that are cheaper than the vendors or small-scale providers that are currently being used. New utility services such as shared water connections or yard connections that allow people to sell water on to their neighbours can have a substantial impact on poverty reduction in those areas compared to expensive vendor water.

Many developing countries are in the process of agreeing or implementing Poverty Reduction Strategy Papers. As such strategies are developed in detail, improved water and sanitation and services for the urban poor are likely to play an important part in the overall strategy.

1.6   Sector challenges

The water and sanitation sectors in low-income countries face substantial challenges. According to the WHO/UNICEF Joint Monitoring Programme, at the turn of the century over 2.4 billion people around the world lacked access to adequate sanitation and over 1.3 billion people lacked access to a safe water supply.

About 40 per cent of the people in Africa still have no access to clean water and improved sanitation, while in India only about 65 per cent of urban dwellers have access to tap water and only 42 per cent have tap water in their premises.

The Water Supply and Sanitation Collaborative Council estimates there is a need to serve an extra one billion urban dwellers in developing countries by the year 2015 - 1.9 billion by the year 2025 - with improved water supply. The challenge is even greater with sanitation services, where 1.1 billion and 2.1 billion extra urban dwellers need to gain access to urban sanitation services by the years 2015 and 2025 respectively (WHO/UNICEF, 2000). According to the World Health Organisation, in order to meet the millennium development goal of 'halving the unserved population by 2015, urban Africa would require an 80% increase in the number of people served (WHO/UNICEF, 2000). This would require on average 6,000 to 8,000 connections every day (WUP, 2003).

The people most affected by inadequate service coverage are low-income households, who often have to spend considerable time collecting water from a variety of sources, some of which may be of dubious quality. The proportion of low-income consumers is also likely to grow as informal settlements grow faster than planned areas.

The high proportion of people using alternative water suppliers and the high prices paid to water vendors (mentioned in Section 1.3) is a clear indication of both the ability and willingness of poor consumers to pay for water. This demonstrates good opportunities for utilities to provide viable improved service options for low-income consumers.

When considering the best means of improving services, we need to be aware of the constraints commonly faced by water utilities, including:

- a supply-driven engineering and management philosophy;

- lack of clear roles and responsibilities between the various stakeholders;

- inadequate strategic and tactical planning;

- bureaucratic controls that inhibit effective management;

- ineffective staffing policy and human resources management;

- high unaccounted-for-water and poor O&M practices;

- low bill collection efficiency leading to high arrears;

- increasing capital costs to obtain water from deteriorating or more distant water sources;

- a lack of staff with the required skills in key areas;

- inadequate management information and systems - a lack of transparency;

- political interference and a lack of a 'willingness to charge' increased water and sanitation tariffs; and

- a lack of incentives to make improvements.

Many utilities are positively addressing such constraints as part of ongoing sector reforms, in some cases using the private sector. Overcoming such constraints mainly involves institutional development, which in turn requires funding from more water revenues. Innovative approaches are required to achieve the twin objectives of improving and extending services whilst ensuring that utilities are financially sustainable. Effective marketing has been used to achieve these two objectives in other sectors and there are good prospects for doing so in the urban water sector. Summary case studies are presented in Section 1.6 on different water sector approaches that have been developed with some success in Asia, Africa and Latin America.

1.7   Marketing sanitation

In this publication, with its focus on city-wide sustainability of a utility, we tend to focus more on water supply than sanitation, particularly with regard to serving the poor. The reason for this is that except in particular situations sewerage with an adequate level of wastewater treatment tends to be unaffordable for those in low-income areas. The challenge of threading gravity-flow sewer pipes at a suitable gradient through illegal, unplanned areas is significantly greater than the extension of water pipes. This is not to say that such areas do not need sanitation, in fact the reverse is true; in public health terms the lowest income householders will benefit disproportionately compared to other areas. However a good means of sanitation for the poor does exist, which is on-plot and on-site sanitation, which is rarely the main responsibility of a water utility.

Because of its individual and discrete characteristics, on-site sanitation does not require the skills of a network utility. Traditionally it has also been co-ordinated by Municipal Departments rather than water utilities. Many professionals dealing with on-site sanitation have also realized the benefits of marketing approaches, whether through 'social marketing' concepts of hygiene promotion, or the conventional marketing of sanitary components such as latrine slabs or pour-flush toilet seals. There are good research-based publications available on marketing discrete low-cost sanitation systems for the poor such as:

- *'Hands on social marketing - a step by step guide'* (1999) by Nedra Kline Weinrich, Sage Publications and

- *'PHAST step by step guide - a participatory approach for the control of diarrhoeal disease'* (1998) a WHO publication by Sara Wood, Ron Sawyer and Mayling Simpson Hebert.

1.8   Examples of innovative approaches in serving the poor

There are many cases of innovative marketing approaches being used to promote water and sanitation services in a collaborative manner in poor communities where both services and prices have been differentiated. Some examples are summarized below from Durban in South Africa, Manila in the Philippines, Guntur and Rajmundry in India, Buenos Aires in Argentina and El Alto in Bolivia.

Durban Metro Water Services, a department of Durban municipality in South Africa, has been offering, promoting and providing different service options in poorer communities since 1993. Box 1.1 summarizes some of the key aspects of their programme.

Box 1.1. Durban Metro Water Service options for poor communities

Durban Metro Water Services, the public water utility in Durban, South Africa, differentiated its water supply to unplanned peri-urban areas by offering:

- water kiosks where people fetch and pay per 20-litre container;
- water kiosk with storage, where people fetch and pay per 20-litre container;
- individual connection with a 200-litre ground tank in the yard, with trickle feed;
- individual house connection with limited pressure through roof tank; and
- individual house connection with full pressure (conventional 24 hour supply).

Durban Metro Water have systematically developed these various options, focusing on the individual connection options, with the price of water to consumers adjusted to suit the costs and then promoted their use amongst poorer communities in newer areas. (Note that this was done prior to the current free water policy for households who consume less than 6M3 per month)

The ground tank concept was first piloted in 1993. The utility supplies the ground tank, a plastic barrel, once the householder is committed to this approach. The tank is often mounted on an old car tyre, to lift it a little above the ground. The tank is covered to prevent contamination and has a float valve to prevent over-filling and wastage. The tank is connected to the water supply main at a manifold or valve cluster situated where it is convenient and cost effective for the utility. In the original concept, the ground tank water system is operated and maintained by a water bailiff, who is selected by the community in the informal settlement, and trained by Durban Metro Water. After training the bailiff looked after about 150 ground tank connections and a water kiosk. Where the consumer had paid their water bill in advance, the water bailiff would open the particular valve once a day until the 200-litre ground tank was filled.

Costs were reduced because householders could pay significantly lower connection charges and there was no need for a full pressure distribution system locally. Bill collection costs were also reduced as there was no need for metering, meter reading or bill delivery.

Private operators have also used innovative options with encouragement from regulators. Box 1.2 highlights interesting developments on concession contracts in Manila in the Philippines. The demands in the contract for increases in service coverage have encouraged the private operators to differentiate service and price to previously unserved low-income consumers, using innovative technologies and approaches with generally successful results.

Box 1.2. Approaches in Manila[1]

In Manila, the Philippines, water supply in the city has been made the responsibility of two private operators who manage water services under a concession contract, supervised by a government regulator. Examples of innovative approaches are briefly described below.

Group taps or yard connections for two to five households where users form groups, register connections, and share the cost of usage. The group is given one mother meter and while it is encouraged to install sub-meters to avoid problems with sharing the costs, some groups opt not to install sub-meters to reduce overall costs further. The group leader collects payments from each member and pays Manila Water.

Bulk water supplies to a community group for on-selling was successfully developed in some settlements where access was difficult. The utility supported the community organization by helping households to complete application forms, etc. With this approach, installation costs as well as the utility's non-revenue water (refer to the glossary for a definition) are minimized with the mother meter located outside the area, usually along main roads, where it can be easily seen and monitored for illegal tapping. The majority of the households in one community paid the costs of pipe installation from the mother meters to the respective households. To minimize project cost, the community coordinated and organized their efforts and contributed their labour (men, women, and children alike) to reduce costs. This project initially provided water to about 250 families. Within the community association there is some 'community' pressure for each household to pay their bills, otherwise the entire community suffers in case of a disconnection for non-payment.

The 'Bayan Tubig' ('water for the community') programme, provides individual household connections in low-income areas at a reduced cost. This programme waives the land title requirement and allows payment of connection fees by instalment over a period of 6 to 12 months (in some cases this has been stretched to 24 months). Technically, this approach involves constructing a conventional underground water main until the narrowness or condition of the access route makes this impratical. From this point the rest of the network is built either above ground or on the ground, partially covered or attached to a wall. This distribution pipe delivers water to a battery or cluster of water meters from where each homeowner makes their own plastic connection, above ground. The programme shows that, given the opportunity, residents of unplanned areas would prefer individual water connections rather than public standposts.

As a result of these initial programmes the researchers observed that the once mostly dilapidated houses have been slowly replaced by structures made of more permanent materials. With more time and water, the women are able to clean their surroundings. Sanitation in the areas covered has also improved as households now have own toilets and bathrooms within their homes.

---

1. Source: An edited version of Inocencio (2002)

Further examples of interesting pilot programmes have occurred in Buenos Aires, where a private operator, Aguas Argentinas, was awarded a concession in 1993 to manage water and sanitation in the capital of Argentina. The concessionaire had a contractual target of achieving full service coverage by the end of the 30-year contract. They began to develop programmes to serve the poor through differentiating services and in particular connection charges. A summary of their approaches is set out in Box 1.3.

Box 1.3. Pilot programmes in Buenos Aires[1]

In a range of projects the utility Aguas Argentinas found that they had to differentiate their projects to suit each low-income community - no single approach suited all situations. Two programmes were particularly interesting:

'The Participative Water Service' projects are described as based on 'direct links' between the residents of the area (via an association or 'leader' or NGO) and Aguas Argentinas. The company found that this 'barter' operating method, with the community providing the construction labour to reduce costs, is only feasible for areas where the idea of community work is already accepted.

The utility generally designs the projects and supervises implementation. To promote subsequent payment, a single invoice is given to the community for a year, to see if they are really willing to pay. Meters are installed for the community bill to limit wastage of water. Typically, one person signs on behalf of the neighbourhood, often designated by minuted community committee meetings. After the trial year is successfully completed, individual billing is introduced, based on an assumed water usage. In one barrio (area), shallow pipes were laid in each alley and just one meter was provided for the entire area.

In this *barrio*, each family was paying their own bill (unmeasured, using average consumption), and there was no connection fee. To reduce costs and promote participation, all the bills for the neighbourhood were given to one community representative for distribution.

Appropriate sanitation in Buenos Aires
A system of shallow sewers was designed for one area because of the high ground water table, using individual or collective septic tanks with liquid effluent transported by a small-diameter PVC network (75mm instead of the 200mm traditionally used in Aguas Argenti-nas secondary networks) with shallow gradients.

Since the plots were too small ($<<100m^2$) to take both a septic tank and a soakaway, the removal of liquid effluent was essential. The cost of the secondary network (the largest item in the sanitation network) was reduced by more than half by the small diameter net-work and the low gradients (less excavation required in areas where the water table is less than one metre below the surface).

The effluent collected is at present evacuated directly into a nearby river: as a result Aguas Argentinas does not charge for the service. When the company network is extended into this area, the collector will simply need to be connected to the mains: the service will then be charged for.

---

1. Based upon Lyonnaise des Eaux (now Ondeo, Suez), 1999, and site investigations by one author (Franceys) as part of a BPD study visit in 1999.

Another example from Bolivia is summarized in Box 1.4. Aguas del Illimani, the private operator in La Paz, El Alto have specific performance targets clearly spelled out in their concession contract which increase annually until the end of the contract in 2026. To achieve these targets the utility sought to use a marketing approach to target services to the needs of the poor.

Box 1.4. Programmes for serving the poor in La Paz, El Alto in Bolivia[1]

Aguas del Illimani, the private operator in La Paz, El Alto has embarked on a series of promotional programmes aimed at raising the company's profile among its users and encouraging wider use of its services, such as:

The **'School Programme'** increases awareness about the water and sewerage system by taking children to visit the treatment plants.

The **'Neighbourhoods Programme'** advises and explains the procedures necessary to obtain a water and sewerage connections in selected neighbourhoods.

The 'IPAS' programme (Peri-urban Initiative for Water and Sanitation) tests innovative approaches for sustained provision of water and sanitation services in the low-income areas of La Paz and El Alto. The project promoted the use of appropriate technologies, sound social intervention methodology, and access to micro-credit mechanisms for construction costs. The micro-credit mechanism also allowed families to develop their credit history and later request subsequent loans for income-generating activities.

At the IPAS project level, community selection procedures were based on the *Demand Responsive Approach*, where communities are consulted beforehand about their interest to participate. Aguas del Illimani first approached different communities in their expansion areas and presented the IPAS project, explaining how it worked and the technology involved. After internal consultation, the community showed its commitment to the project by presenting signatures of at least 70 per cent of its dwellers.

As a result of savings in installation costs and also as an incentive for participating communities, the utility offered a discounted connection fee which is about 60 per cent of the original connection fee, payable in 60 monthly instalments in the water bill at no interest.

---

1. An edited version of Vargas, M., Incentives for utilities to serve the urban poor El Alto, Bolivia, in Incentives for utilities to serve the urban poor, Franceys, R, ed, IHE for WSSCC, 2002

Finally, an example from Guntur, in India, where marketing research has been undertaken by the Administrative Staff College of India (ASCI), is briefly described in Box 1.5.

In the Indian cases the utilities have adopted marketing-type approaches to serve poor communities, whether this has been done consciously or otherwise. They have developed appropriate products or service options that they have promoted to selected people (potential customers) at viable prices, using appropriate processes in selected places where there are demands for service improvements. In doing so the utility has enhanced its presence as a consumer-orientated organization. They have therefore been addressing the 7Ps of marketing, a tool that helps providers get the 'marketing mix' right for each situation. This provides a useful framework for developing, promoting and providing different options, refer to section 2.6 on the marketing mix

Box 1.5. Marketing initiatives in Guntur, India[1]

The poor in Guntur and Rajhamundry in Andhra Pradesh, India, depend mainly on free public standposts and tankers provided by the Municipal Corporations for their potable water (Narender and Chary, 2002). The water supplied through public standposts is quite inadequate to cover the needs of the majority of the households.

A significant proportion of the poor have expressed their willingness to make individual connections and were prepared to pay the required monthly charges. However, they were discouraged by the Corporation policy that demands a one-off connection fee of about Rs.5000-7000 (US$100-$130). As a result, many poor households were excluded from individual coverage by the water system; they were in effect not allowed to enter the 'shop'. This has resulted in a proliferation of illegal connections.

During long discussions with the Corporations as part of marketing research, however, the leaders of the Municipal Corporations realized the need to increase the coverage of water services to the poor through innovative approaches.

In 2002 the leadership of the Municipal Corporations made significant efforts to remove the entry barrier. They have not only lowered the connection charges as prescribed by Government norms, but also allowed the poor to pay these one-off charges in two or three instalments. They have also reduced or waived the associated supervision charges for executing the work. The mayors and commissioners have visited several slums, conducted public meetings and issued on-the-spot connection approvals to the willing households. As a result of these sustained efforts, the number of poor households with individual connections has gone up significantly in these cities in the past year. In another variation poor households were also encouraged to form groups of six to eight households to access a single connection to reduce the burden of connection and tariff charges.

The Municipal Corporations have also experimented with marketing ideas such as promoting (advertising) new connections in 'Saturday connection camps' and through offering the poorest household in a group of ten a special 'bargain' low-cost connection. The experiences of Guntur and Rajhamundry demonstrate that the city governments are becoming aware of and are willing to adopt marketing approaches to increase water services particularly to the poor.

1. Source: Drafted by S.Chary, 2002

Chapter 2

Marketing water services for all consumer groups

2.1 Introduction and summary

This chapter summarizes the problems with the conventional predict and provide approaches to water service provision. It then describes a number of suitable marketing approaches and how they can be applied to the urban water sector in low and middle-income countries. This is intended to provide sufficient detail to enable governments, regulators and civil society institutions to encourage water utilities and municipalities to use or adapt these approaches to provide services for their various consumer groups, including the poor.

The marketing approaches that are advocated include the *'customer value chain'*, which is the process of *knowing, targeting, selling and servicing* existing and potential customers. This provides a framework for initial pilot projects aimed at serving the poor. The key aspects are as follows:

Knowing and understanding all consumer groups

If utilities and regulators have a thorough understanding of the experiences, perceptions and preferences for service improvements of all consumer groups, then there are much better prospects for utility initiatives to be more effective and efficient in the longer term.

The poor often miss out in the allocation of resources and market segmentation can assist with effective planning for improved services for low-income areas, as well as for other consumer groups. Market segmentation entails showing the location of the key consumer groups (by house type, income level etc) on up to date utility maps, so that all market segments are considered when the utility is planning for service improvements in the short, medium and longer term. The use of GIS which are computerized Geographical Information Systems can provide valuable information for this planning process.

There are a variety of consumer survey techniques in common use. Enumerator-completed questionnaires and focus group discussions are particularly useful and are a generally reliable means for obtaining accurate data. Governments, regulators and utilities need to ensure that sufficient data on the various water consumer groups is being collected and acted upon using good performance measurement techniques, in order to support effective decision making.

Targeting low income consumers

Funds for improving services in poorly served areas are often limited, so careful thought is required on where to target resources. Effective targeting or prioritizing of future investments and efforts for low income areas is best done considering:

- **The selection of priority areas** on the basis of agreed objectives, using the best available information about the needs and demands of consumers for different service and payment options, together with utility performance data against key indicators.

- **The development of feasible service, payment and management options** based on lessons learnt elsewhere and locally. Innovations should be considered such as the use of local water storage tanks where water supplies are intermittent. Option development should be guided by the principles of maximising revenues but also providing the best feasible supply to poorly served areas until the utility can provide better services (such as house connections) in those areas.

- **Assessing consumer demands** for existing and new service options using appropriate techniques such as willingness to pay surveys or PREPP (see book 3). Such studies will inform the likely future take up of different options and the scope for increasing tariffs, which is invaluable for utility financial planning.

- **Exploring opportunities for working with other stakeholders** such as CBOs, NGOs and small water enterprises is important when working in informal settlements, because utilities often do not have all the resources and skills to work in such areas.

When initial pilot programmes for working in low income areas are being developed, the targeting of which areas to work in is likely to be less rigorous. Larger programmes should include more systematic targeting.

Selling and servicing low-income consumers

Once a utility has targeted areas where it wants to improve services, established partnerships with other stakeholders, and assessed demand for new options, it needs to consider how it can sell and provide service options on a sustainable basis, as part of the final step in the customer value chain. One useful marketing framework for developing appropriate strategies is the marketing mix. This mix will be different from situation to situation, but will always contain elements of product, price, promotion, place, people, process and presence, or *the 7Ps of marketing*.

The 7Ps is a simple marketing framework that can easily be used in workshops and meetings as a means of capturing the ideas of concerned staff and stakeholders. More guidance on providing improved services is included in the section on strategic marketing.

The strategic marketing framework

To ensure that a marketing approach to serving the poor can be replicated across many low-income areas in a city with long-term sustainability ensured, a strategic marketing approach is required. What can be made to work with special effort in a few low-income areas in a city can have a different impact on a utility's operations when it has to be scaled up across the entire city, particularly when 30-60 per cent of the population may be living in informal low-income housing areas.

There are a number of reasons why, after initial piloting work, marketing plans for urban water services needs to be reasonably strategic and comprehensive, including the following:

- Utilities need to feel confident that if they offer new options and services, then they can provide them on a sustainable and reliable basis.

- Precedence and equity are also important considerations., so rational and fair targeting or prioritising of new investments is required.

Strategic marketing is a comprehensive approach for organizations to make the case for investment through understanding the perceptions and preferences of different customer groups and their willingness to pay for different types of services. This leads to the development of viable business plans for targeting and promoting appropriate service, payment and management options that can be provided reliably to each of those customer groups or market segments at appropriate prices.

The main questions to be addressed in the strategic marketing process for urban water services are

- *Where are we now?*

- *Where do we want to be?*

- *How might we get there?*

- *How do we ensure success?*

These questions can form a natural structure for a strategic marketing plan or utility business plan. If Government departments and regulators can encourage utilities to utilise such marketing approaches, then there are better opportunities for accelerated service improvements. They can also utilise the information generated from such strategies, in order to fulfil their own objectives, such as ensuring value for money from investments and reviewing progress on poverty reduction.

2.2   Conventional predict and provide approaches

The case studies from a variety of countries in Chapter 1 show that it is possible to serve the poor, even in informal housing areas, using innovative approaches. But a persistent cause of lack of action is the difficulties of making the case to key stakeholders for more investment to implement improvements, based upon an older style, engineering-biased understanding of water supply.

The conventional approach to overcoming the service gap has been to invest large amounts of money in bulk water supply infrastructure to ensure a sufficient quantity of water is available. The methodology involves predicting the likely population within a reasonable time horizon, taking the standard design criteria of litres of water used per person per day, adding on for commercial, institutional and industrial users, and providing treatment works and transmission mains sufficient to deliver that water to the city.

This approach often fails to notice that half the water delivered is lost through leakage and theft whilst the other half is sold to consumers at a price below the operating costs of supplying that water, with little notice taken of recovering capital costs. Experience also shows that a fair proportion of consumers do not pay their water bills even when they are below cost. This approach also ignores the fact that those operating costs may be unacceptably high because of inefficient equipment and staffing. It also fails to address the point that there has to be investment in distribution networks to get the water to where people live and that the 'illegality' of slums is not a sufficient problem to prohibit water supply to the poor.

Similarly for sanitation, utilities have tended to look at the costs of comprehensive drainage plans and given up in despair before they even consider the concomitant costs of wastewater treatment. 'Knowing' that on-plot and on-site sanitation solutions could pollute the groundwater and also knowing that different government organizations are usually responsible for non-sewerage sanitation, utilities have tended to give up on the unserved population and focus on subsidizing sewerage services to the commercial core of the city.

Moving from the above common scenario to a demand-responsive, customer-oriented approach therefore requires institutional development as well as a marketing approach. It will still require an element of predict and provide, as the water industry is a capital-intensive, long-term industry. But in particular it will require a new, innovative, creative and partnership-based approaches to serving the urban poor.

2.3   The marketing approach

A marketing approach is of particular relevance to the water sector in developing countries because household consumers in urban centres often obtain water from numerous alternative providers and sources. At one level, water utilities 'compete' with alternative water from untreated sources. Across a typical city private vendors, individual household on-selling, family and institutional boreholes, hand-dug wells, streams, rainwater and springs complement the conventional utility water, thus illustrating the water market in action.

These 'alternative supplies' that often supplement or substitute direct utility-provided water are accessed through informal human and physical networks. Although often unregulated, unreliable and costly, people use them regularly either through necessity or choice. At some level all these sources of water supply attract reasonably 'loyal' customers and represent degrees of competition to utilities that are required to operate in the same market.

So it is clear that competition exists in the domestic market and that city dwellers do not always automatically look to the utility to provide services. If utilities are to capture neglected or new markets then a customer-focused, effective strategic marketing strategy needs to be developed and implemented.

Successful international companies, including those in the water sector, have found that a key to success is having a clear customer focus and by striving to provide good quality services. By seeking to maximize the numbers of satisfied customers, a water utility can gain many benefits. The most obvious of which is that a utility should receive less complaints resulting in less interference from politicians on operational aspects. In addition, a customer services focus can improve financial sustainability in two ways:

- customers who are satisfied with the service they are receiving are more likely to accept and pay reasonable water charges; and

- increased numbers of paying customers, where there are cost-reflective tariffs, generate higher revenue and sustainable returns on investment.

The increased revenues can then be invested in improving services, which in turn increases customer satisfaction levels and so a cycle of continuing improvement can develop.

Managing water services (and sanitation) successfully is like any other business where the responsible organization seeks to: keep customers satisfied, increase market share, and maximize revenues. In Box 2.1 examples of evidence of how good business performance is linked to market orientation are provided.

Box 2.1. Importance of marketing orientation[1]

The influence of marketing on higher or sustained business performance has been the subject of a number of studies. The conclusions from two of those studies are:

- Hooley and Lynch (1985) examined 1504 British companies and concluded that the high-performing organizations were characterized by a significantly greater market orientation, strategic direction, and concern with product quality than the 'also rans'.

- Narver and Slater (1990) focused on the marketing orientation of the senior managers in 140 North American strategic business units (SBUs) and identified a very strong relationship between marketing orientation and profitability. They also found that the *highest degree of market orientation* was manifested by managers of the *most profitable companies.*

---

1. Source: Wilson and Gilligan (1997)

Marketing is about satisfying customers. Jones (1989) has defined marketing as: 'The management process responsible for identifying, anticipating and satisfying customer requirements profitably'.

The implications of this statement are that ongoing communication with existing and potential customers is required to check the effectiveness of efforts to identify, anticipate and satisfy customer requirements profitably. Some government water-supply organizations may be uncomfortable with the term 'profitably', but few would argue with the need to generate sufficient funds for future investment.

A water utility with a marketing-orientated philosophy would have its entire operations, its personnel and its technical systems geared to providing improved customer satisfaction and contributing to meeting its financial objectives. Marketing can also be viewed as a management process. Typically, it involves (adapted from Wilson and Gilligan, 1997):

- investigating customer demand for different product options;

- identifying groups of customers whose requirements could be better satisfied;

- developing reliable products or service options to meet changing demands;

- pricing the product at a level which the market will bear and which will meet its financial objectives; and

- making the product or service available through channels accessible to the consumer, promoting the product or service so that a desired unit or revenue or volume of demand is achieved.

This process of incorporating marketing approaches throughout an organization can be termed Strategic Marketing where it takes an all-embracing, long-term view as discussed in Section 2.7.

But is marketing really necessary for a monopoly supplier of a basic need? Many water utilities, in principle, now appreciate that the 'Customer is King' and that they should therefore be treated as 'the fountain of knowledge'. For any business to survive, including enterprises that strive to deliver a 'social good', it is important to build enduring profitable relationships with current and potential customers. Only then can the direct provider be effective and efficient.

A useful concept to achieve this effectiveness and efficiency is the 'Customer Value Chain', which can be described as to *know, target, sell and service* knowledge' (Sage, 2000).

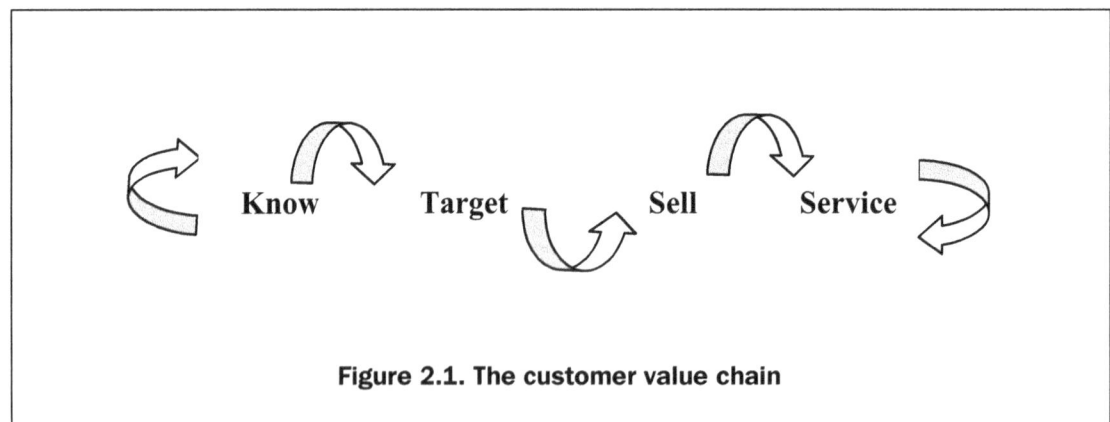

Figure 2.1. The customer value chain

This concept is increasingly used in the commercial sector, and in the context of the water sector, it involves the following:

Know and understand the different customer and potential customer groups, including their attitudes, coping strategies, perceptions, preferences and their willingness to sustain payment for improved services. Key methods for getting to know water users are questionnaire surveys, focus group discussions, customer consultative committees and local observation.

Target specific areas or customer groups (market segments) such as: commercial customers, domestic customers in low, middle and high-income areas, with appropriate service options such as house connections, yard taps and water kiosks, at appropriate price levels.

Sell options using suitable promotion techniques and plans. This will often require careful planning and implementation, particularly when dealing with groups who use alternative water supplies or who have unauthorized pipe connections and do not currently pay at all.

Services should be provided to a high quality standard, delivered through a balance of people, processes and technology by knowledgeable staff. To provide such a standard of service requires the utilities to adopt a programme of continual organizational improvement centred around 'the customer'. Servicing the customer will mean, for example, offering payment options to suit their particular needs.

The customer value chain concept is used in Sections 2.4 to 2.6 as a framework for developing marketing approaches in the urban water sector context.

2.4   Knowing and understanding all consumer groups

The staff of a water utility need to have a good knowledge of the different consumer groups if they are to be able to do their work in a manner that increases customer satisfaction and service coverage. There has been a tendency for utility/municipal staff to assume that they already know what the consumer wants. Experience in the business sector shows that good quality information about consumer perceptions, experiences and preferences is required if real improvements are to be made.

Such quality information can only be learned through well-planned interactions with current and potential customers, using methods such as questionnaire surveys, focus group discussions (such as PREPP) and semi-structured interviews. Summaries of such consumer information are also very useful for governments and regulators who are concerned with assessing utility performance and services to consumers.

It is important to gather data on all the key consumer groups in a city or town, so that appropriate marketing strategies can be developed that balance the needs and demands of each group. The next section, on market segmentation, considers how best to define these groups or market segments. This is followed by an overview of different survey techniques.

Market segmentation

It is not possible to get to know individual water customers, except perhaps for the few largest consumers or perhaps the constant complainers. The marketing approach therefore divides up customers into a manageable number of groups of customers, a process that is known as 'segmentation.' This dividing up for conventional marketing can follow 'social class' lines that incorporate aspects of income or it can follow 'lifestyle' patterns that have been found to be better predictors of consumer behaviour for particular products. Segmentation has been defined as 'the process of identifying groups of customers with enough characteristics in common to make possible the design and presentation of a product or service each group needs' (Heskett, 1986). The concept of market segmentation is based on the belief that 'people with broadly similar economic, social and lifestyle characteristics tend to congregate in particular neighbourhoods and exhibit similar patterns of purchasing behaviour and outlook' (Wilson and Gilligan, 1997).

One of the main reasons for market segmentation is to understand consumer perspectives and develop viable plans to serve the specific needs and demands of all consumer groups, and thus avoid missing out some groups, which otherwise often occurs. If we are to 'target specific customer groups or market segments with suitable service and payment options, at appropriate price levels', as is proposed in the 'customer value chain' , then we need to think carefully about how we define our consumer groups or segment the market.

Selection of criteria for market segmentation in the water sector should consider factors such as:

- Is market segmentation feasible and practical using the selected criteria?

- Will the segments be sufficiently unique to be distinguishable from each other?

- Will the segments be adequately stable so that their present and future characteristics can be predicted with a sufficient degree of confidence?

In many cities in developing countries, needs and conditions differ substantially from one neighbourhood to the next. For example, viable service options in higher income low-density housing areas (such as in-house connections with full internal plumbing) will be quite different from those in informal settlements. It is not realistic, therefore, for the water utility to provide a uniform service to customers whose needs, wants and willingness to pay are so different. It is for this reason that market segmentation can be used as a means of targeting viable options to appropriate user groups.

For urban water and sewerage services, potential variables for segmentation that have emerged from strategic marketing research include:

- the type of dwelling and location (e.g. bungalows, flats, informal housing and mixed) which can serve as a proxy for income;

- roofing materials;

- housing densities (e.g. high, medium and low-density); and

- socio-economic information using recent census data (where available).

Based on research in East Africa and India, a suitable and practical criterion for segmentation that emerged is the 'type of dwelling or building'. In many urban areas of developing countries, the type of dwelling that people live in is generally a reflection of their socio-economic status. The people who live in slums and other informal settlements are generally the poor. Those in well-planned residential estates tend to be the more affluent in the population or living in housing provided by government for its employees. This may of course not apply in every case, but we are seeking a planning framework that is 'good enough' for effective decision-making.

Table 2.1 illustrates the use of 'type of dwelling' as a basis for market segmentation that was used in the Guntur Strategic Marketing Plan (SMP) from India. It is clear that income levels vary substantially between each of these segments.

Use of type of dwelling or type of building criteria for market segmentation is relatively easy to implement in the field, since dwellings are visible and can easily fit into one of the specified market segments. Another advantage of this type of segmentation is that viable technical and management options for water provision can be provided to suit different market segments on the basis of type of dwelling.

Table 2.1. Guntur average household income by market segment[1]

Market segment	Average household income (estimated in Rs.*)
Bungalows	11,765
Independent houses in planned areas	7,833
Independent houses in unplanned areas	4,625
Flats in planned areas	10,078
Flats in unplanned areas	11,180
Slums having some water supply coverage	2,113
Slums having no water supply coverage	605

1. Source: Narender Chary and Sansom, 2004
    *Note: the exchange rate is Rs.42 = US$1

If there are doubts about segmenting the water market in a particular city by house type or roof type, then it is possible to compare sample areas with socio-economic data that may be available from a recent census. If there is a clear correlation between, say, house type and factors such income levels and current water service options, then segmentation can proceed using this criteria.

Use of segmented plans and data

An example of a market segmentation plan for an area of Arusha in Tanzania is shown in Figure 2.2. The validity of the segmented areas would of course need to be verified on the ground. Such plans are useful for:

*   consumer survey purposes - ensuring that each consumer group and area is adequately represented in the survey;

*   developing and implementing marketing strategies for each segment and area;

*   linking the location of water infrastructure and service levels with each market segment and area; and

*   planning service improvements to poorly served areas or informal settlements.

Note that people living in one unplanned settlement may have quite different service levels, perceptions, and demands from another unplanned settlement in the city. So it is important to sample each area.

Whatever method of segmentation is chosen, the data to support it should be readily available and there should be correlation with what is visible on the ground. It is for this reason that housing types or roof materials are perhaps the easiest means of segmentation.

One means of illustrating the resulting segmentation of present and potential consumer groups is through 'social mapping.' An example of a social map from Bolivia is shown in Figure 2.3. Data obtained from a consumer survey was collected and presented on the basis of the identified market segments in order to provide useful decision-support information.

Sample market segmentation plan for Arusha, Tanzania

Key :

U = Unplanned area
R = Residential houses in planned areas
F = Flats
Ind = Industrial
Inst = Institutional
S = Shops/Commerce

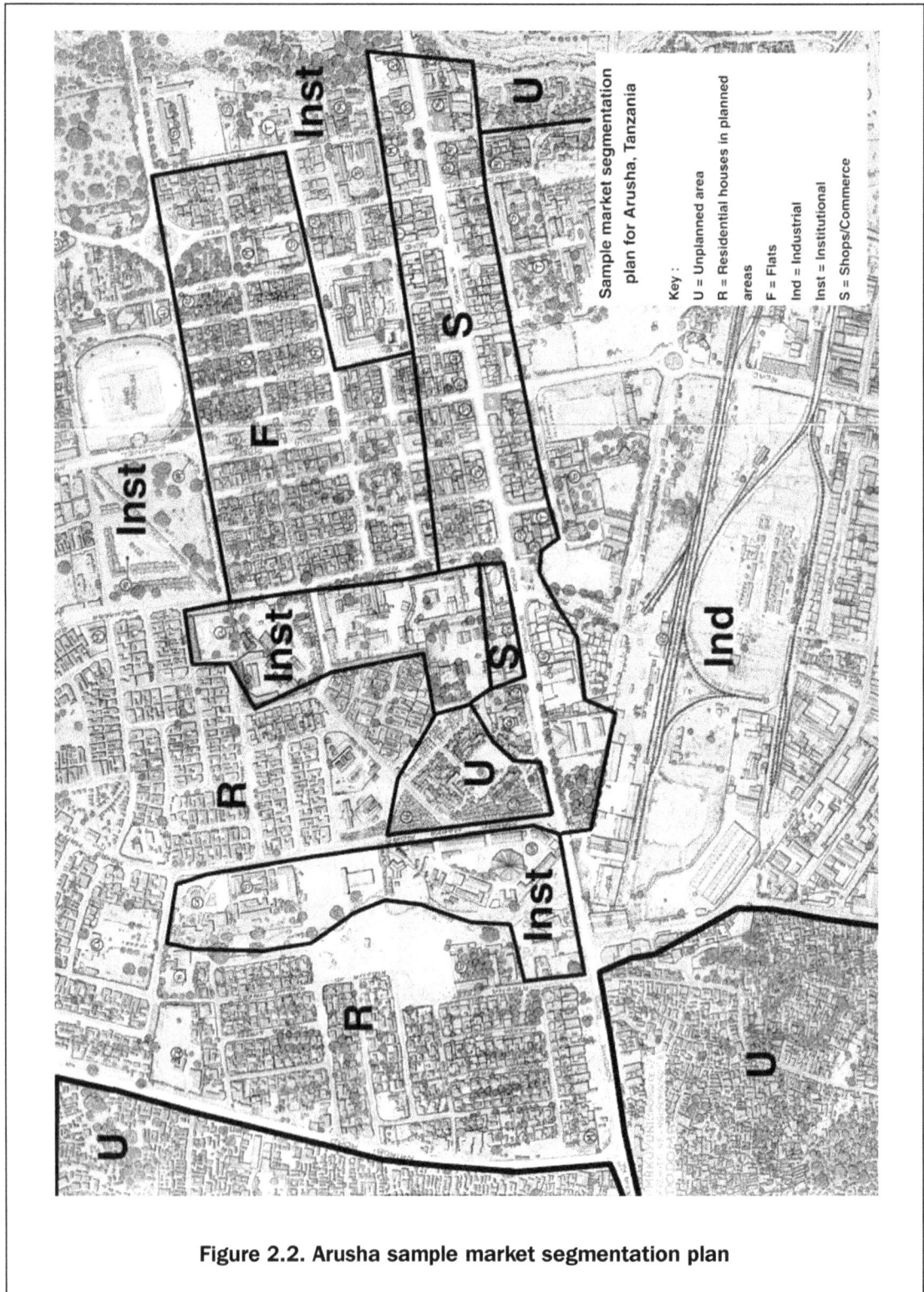

Figure 2.2. Arusha sample market segmentation plan

Use of GIS

A significant challenge when seeking to improve water services to informal settlements, is obtaining comprehensive information on precisely where all the poor and unserved houses are located. Updating existing maps by manually surveying all the new houses and drawing the new buildings on the utility maps is a laborious task that often does not get done regularly.

AGUAS DEL ILLIMANI

POOR HOUSEHOLDS BY CENSAL AREAS
LA PAZ AND EL ALTO

PROPORTION OF POOR HOUSEHOLDS

5.7% - 24% Low
24.1% - 42.3% Moderate
42.4% - 60.7% Medium
60.8% - 79.0% Severe
79.1% - 98% High

AIRPORT

N

Poor Households : In funtion of three rancks than assume the intensity index I(NBI)k this are:
- Marginal Poors: Average households with an insatisfaction level in their basic needs of 85 % in
relation with minimum living levels (standard).
- Indigente Poor : Households than cover only the 45% of minimum living conditions (standard).
- Moderate Poors: 25% of insatisfaction conditions (standard)

Figure 2.3. Social map of La Paz and El Alto, Bolivia

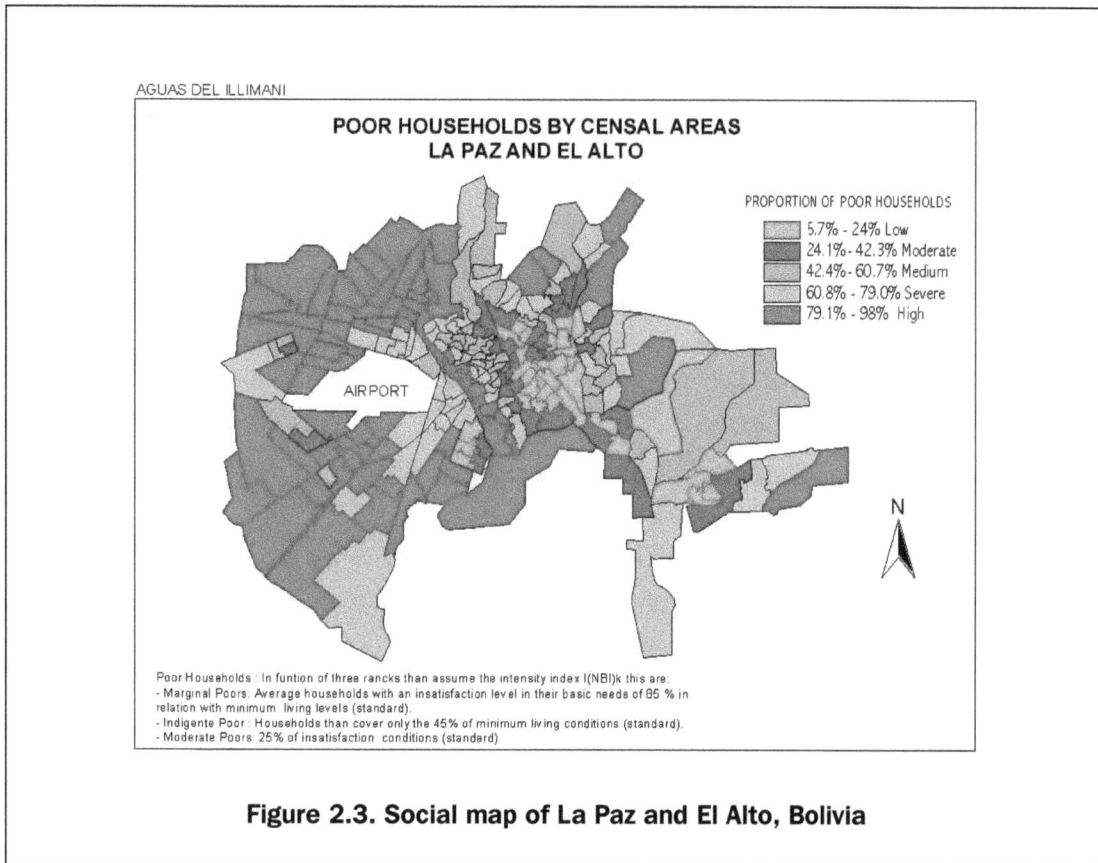

A number of utilities, for example in Kampala and Durban, are now using GIS (Geographical Information Systems), which are based on aerial photographs of the utility service area. The photographs are digitally stored on the utility computers and can be used to produce accurate maps to the required scale for whatever purpose. Some of the key features of the GIS used at Durban Metro Water in South Africa are briefly discussed in Box 2.2.

It is clear from Durban Metro Water's GIS experience that having such valuable and up to date information at a 'press of few buttons' has a number advantages:

• Good access to data and management information summaries about different consumer groups (or market segments) including those in poorer areas, which enables well informed and quick decision making;

• Where repairs, maintenance work or new connections are required, key technical information about the existing water infrastructure is readily available.

• Enables effective strategic planning for providing services to unserved areas.

• Enables more accurate and speedy responses to customer requests and complaints.

Such benefits are best achieved by obtaining and maintaining good quality data on the GIS. Other utilities and government may, therefore, wish to consider this approach.

Overview of consumer survey techniques

Consumer and demand-assessment surveys enable a water supply organization to collect data that will be used:

Box 2.2. GIS at Durban Metro Water[1]

Durban Metro Water (now called Ethekwini Water) in South Africa have developed their GIS (Geographical Information Systems) in recent years to enhance the management of water and sanitation services to over 3 million consumers.

The aerial photographic surveys for the GIS are redone each year to produce up to date digitized maps of all properties, at a "relatively cheap cost". Such maps are very useful, particularly for locating recently constructed properties in informal settlements, that may otherwise be unknown to utility service providers. The Durban GIS system has more than 30 different layers of relevant information that can be shown on its digitized computer maps including the following:

- The precise location of all connected and unconnected properties
- The location of all water and sewer pipes and utility facilities
- The location of all water meters (to enable quick meter reading)
- Records of repairs over the years on each water main
- Links to each customer's water consumption
- Links to each customer's payment records
- Links to customer complaint records
- Unique numbers for all properties (to enable the speedy location of properties and maintenance problems)
- Roads and street furniture
- Links to the design or 'as built' drawings of each pipeline

These various layers can be turned on or off to suite the purpose of the member of staff using the GIS, and printouts can be made of the map area under consideration at an appropriate scale.

Durban Metro Water has 700,000 connections and it has connected 98,000 new customers in the last 8 years. Each connected property has a unique property number that can be quoted by the customer from which the utility can locate that property immediately using the GIS

---

1. Source: Presentation by Neil McLeod, Head of Ethekwini Water and summarised by Kevin Sansom in December 2003.

- to understand the different customer and potential customer groups, including their attitudes, practices, perceptions and preferences, as well as water use and buying habits, so that affordable service improvements can be devised;

- to develop new service options or modify existing service options and carry out service differentiation;

- to estimate future demand;

- to estimate affordability to pay for services;

- to establish maximum willingness-to-pay levels for service options; and

- to enables the water utility to develop a customer care programme and monitor the progress of customer service initiatives.

Many organizations use the traditional method of monitoring complaints and compliments in order to keep track of the views of their customers. By being proactive in finding out about customer concerns and taking prompt action on customers' complaints, the organization saves, rather than spends money.

Depending on the objective of the survey, the types of consumer being surveyed and the intended use of the data, an organization may decide to use one or several of these research methods for data collection:

- Self-completed questionnaires

- Enumerator-completed questionnaires

- Face-to-face interviews

- Focus group discussions

- Telephone surveys

Enumerator-completed questionnaires are particularly useful and are a generally reliable means for obtaining accurate data both for consumer surveys and willingness-to-pay surveys. A two-page consumer survey questionnaire for water services and coping strategies in informal settlements is included in Annex 2. This survey format was field-tested in five towns in Uganda in June 2003 and it provides independent information against key indicators which are discussed further in Chapter 3.

Focus group discussions are appropriate for obtaining good in-depth qualitative data and improving dialogue with groups such as communities in informal settlements.

Experience in the UK has shown that disputes can arise where the regulator and the private water utilities have both conducted consumer surveys and each questions the validity of the others' survey data.

In response to this problem, the regulator, utilities and the relevant government department have jointly commissioned a variety of consumer surveys with specific terms of reference to avoid potential disputes over data validity. This idea is potentially transferable elsewhere.

Focus group discussions and the 'PREPP' approach

People living in informal settlements may have limited trust in or experience of dealing with public utilities. Focus group discussions (FGD) offer an effective technique for a utility to develop an understanding of the attitudes, practices, perceptions and preferences of its customers. It can also be the basis for ongoing dialogue.

A refinement of focus group discussions, PREPP - 'Participation, Ranking, Experience, Perception and Partnership', has been developed and tested in East Africa and India (Book 3, Coates et al., 2004). This approach provides a reasonably rapid method of directly addressing some of the issues that arise from miscommunication between the utility and the poor. Too often that relationship is one where low-income consumers do not see themselves as valued customers now or in the future.

PREPP is a practical method for utilities to consult low-income consumers. Developed with the assistance of utility engineers, social scientists and economists and piloted in low-income communities in Kenya, Uganda, Zambia and India, PREPP is grounded in the belief that a utility and a low-income consumer can have a mutually profitable relationship.

The costed option ranking stage of PREPP also provides valuable information on user demand for the targeting phase. Guidance on the use of this very useful and streamlined approach is described in Book 3.

2.5   Targeting low-income consumers

Targeting or prioritizing future investments and efforts is best done on the basis of agreed objectives, using the best available information about the needs and demands of consumers for different service and payment options. The following sections consider the selection of priority areas and the challenges of working in informal settlements. This is followed by the development of feasible service, payment and management options and a brief discussion of demand assessment techniques that provide valuable information for the selection of the preferred service options. Opportunities for working with other stakeholders such as CBOs, NGOs and small water enterprises are considered as a means of maximizing the effectiveness of services for low income consumer groups.

Selecting priority areas

As funds are invariably limited, utilities need to agree which areas are a priority for improved services. Market segmentation plans, utility performance data, as well as the results of consumer surveys and demand assessment surveys provide an effective and impartial basis for selecting the priority areas, thus avoiding the potential criticism of favouritism during the selection process.

As many low-income consumers often live in informal or unplanned areas that typically experience inadequate services, these are often likely to be priority areas for improvement. Governments with clear poverty reduction strategies are likely to encourage utilities and other stakeholders to improve services in such areas.

Initially, when comprehensive city-wide data may not be available, a utility may want to target certain low-income areas to pilot work based on limited information. This is a sensible strategy initially, because there is a need to 'learn by doing', but ultimately when planning for city-wide services this needs to be done based on more comprehensive survey information.

The needs of consumer groups in other market segments, such as middle and high-income residential areas, also needs to be catered for as part of the utility's strategic planning, and this is discussed in Section 2.8.

Working in informal settlements

Informal housing settlements, slums, compounds, or peri-urban areas provide viable though often unexplored revenue bases for utilities. The fact is that many of the consumers who are not served directly by the utility live in such areas and continue to have inadequate access to basic water and sanitation services. This means that they need to obtain water from elsewhere, often paying inflated prices for water of poor quality. For the community and household this means that related social and economic factors, including chronic health problems, are made worse. For the utility a sizeable percentage of its potential revenue base remains untapped. This need not be the case.

The following statements are often made to explain why informal settlements are left without utility provided services:

'the poor can't pay'

'they (the poor) are looked after by donors and NGOs'

'we (the utility) are only just managing to serve the rest of the city without supplying people who are living on land illegally'

The challenge for utilities and governments is to change the assumptions that exist about informal settlements and their potential for revenue. This means recognising the scope for growth in these areas and devising simple and achievable methods for capturing people's willingness to pay for services.

Working in informal settlements has opportunities and particular features. Where water is often a scarce commodity and prices are high, people develop coping strategies to ensure a reasonable supply to suit their household needs. Water is both a social and an economic issue, central to the daily pattern of people's lives. If a utility aims to capture the informal settlement market, it must understand the perceptions and preferences of the people who live there, perhaps more than for any other social group that they may wish to attract. This can only be achieved by meeting the residents face-to-face and establishing meaningful and continued dialogue with them.

Key challenges that are common in informal settlements are the limited ability or willingness-to-pay of many users, and the restricted space available for infrastructure such as water mains. It is therefore necessary to be more creative in developing appropriate service, payment and management options.

Developing options

For those people who receive good full pressure 24 hour water services, the service options to consider promoting may seem somewhat limited. Effective water utilities, however, seek to introduce viable options wherever they can, such as payment and service options, in order to improve customer satisfaction. The potential to introduce more options increases substantially in situations where services are currently intermittent and/ or inadequate, particularly in developing countries.

Some of the potential improved service options that can be offered to consumers compared to typical existing water sources are illustrated in Table 2.2. The existing water sources are listed in the left-hand column and potential options as part of incremental improvements are in the right-hand column.

Table 2.2. Examples of existing and improved water options in informal settlements

Typical existing water sources	Potential improved service options
· Unregulated water kiosks · Handcart vendors (expensive) · Unauthorised connections · Public standposts from which little or no revenue is collected · Contaminated pools or rivers · Distant springs or boreholes · Seasonal dug wells	· Utility-supported private water kiosks · Regulated small-scale providers or vendors · Community-managed kiosks · Community-managed local water distribution pipes · Shared water connections with on-selling to neighbours · Individual connections · Prepaid metered kiosks · Water kiosks with storage tanks

Such incremental improvements are often a more realistic process, particularly where a utility is trying to improve services to as many people as possible. Whatever options are developed, key objectives for the utility are generally to recoup investments and increase coverage.

The following sections on service options, payment options and management options give examples of successful innovative approaches to improving services from around the world. If utilities are to offer more of such options to existing and potential customers, then they will invariably need to be more flexible in terms of their design standards and procedures, as part of an effective marketing strategy.

Service options

Many water utilities provide limited options such as house connections and standpipes or water kiosks, but the scope for introducing more options to improve customer satisfaction is considerable. A key aspect to improving customer services is development of different service options that can be used and address the demands of consumers in different market segments. These options should be both technically feasible and financially viable. They should be priced according to peoples' willingness to pay and should also be environmentally feasible.

In technical terms in the context of utility provision, water service options may generally be grouped into seven basic categories:

- **Individual house connections** with various pressure regimes and frequency of water supply. There may be a variety of means of connecting to the water mains, by conventional buried pipe, possibly metered, or through informal connections to an individual manifold or meter some distance from the dwelling. Water is obtained from a tap in the house which is usually the desired level of service.

- **Individual yard connections** at various pressure regimes and frequency of supply, where water is obtained from a tap outside the house. The house is unlikely to have internal plumbing.

- **Shared group connections** with a few households or a 'street' sharing one connection at various pressure regimes and frequency of supply in order to minimize connection charges and any fixed standing charges

- **Bulk supply connections** where the utility sells water through a bulk meter at special rates to a community or private contractor, possibly with on-site storage capacity, for on-selling through a private distribution network to household connections or even to water kiosks.

- **Water kiosks**, essentially communal/public waterpoints, technically similar to 'standposts' where people buy water. A water kiosk may be sheltered (with a structure) or open, and may include storage and/or bathing facilities. A utility, a private operator or a community group may manage the water kiosk and sell water at a predetermined price per container, although different payment methods may be adopted.

- **Standposts** are communal/public points where water is collected by many people. Standposts, as opposed to kiosks, are usually unmanned and there is no direct charge for the water provided (particularly in South Asia).

- **Supply by vendors** who may use various modes of transporting water such as bicycles, handcarts, animal-drawn carts and motorised delivery vehicles (trucks) to deliver water to consumers.

- **Supply by water tankers.** The utility or a private provider may deliver water to an area using a water tanker, especially in cases of water shortages.

For each of the above basic service options, different payment mechanisms and management systems can be adopted. Apart from these basic service options, others can be developed depending on the particular circumstances faced by respective water utilities. The basic options can also be modified to suit customer requirements. A broader range of water supply options that have been used around the world are listed in Table 2.3.

Table 2.3. Water service options for selected variables in urban areas

Location of water delivery point	Max 100m away	Max 25m away	Yard	House
Pressure	As in conventional network	Roof (first storey)	Ground	Trickle feed
Hours of supply	24, 12, 9, 6, 2 hours			
Type of dwellings	Bungalows and maisonettes (with internal plumbing)	Flats (with internal plumbing)	1,2 or 3-roomed dwellings (without internal plumbing)	Dwellings in informal settlements
	Commercial premises	Single or two-storey	Multi-storey	Tenement rooms/flats
Water point delivery	Multiple taps	Single tap	Water kiosks	Valve clusters with hosepipe offtakes
	Standposts	Standpost vendors	Locked shared standposts	Machine dispensers
	Storage standposts	Smart card or pre-payment meters	Neighbourhood reselling	Handcart vendors
	Flow restrictors / trickle Flow	Storage containers	Shared connections	Water regulator CSIR
	Site storage	Area storage		Tanker vendors

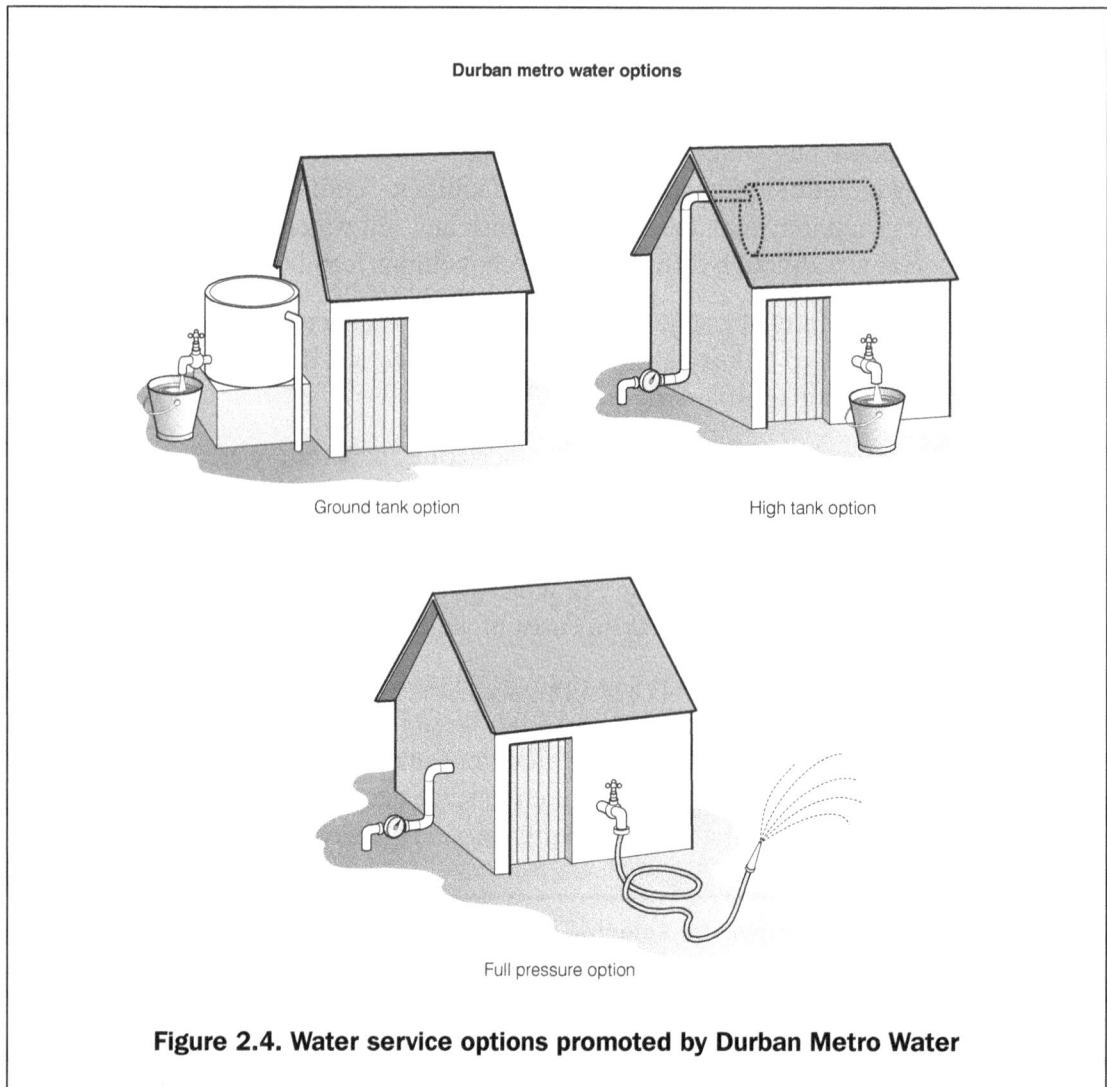

Figure 2.4. Water service options promoted by Durban Metro Water

In developing service options that are suitable for their consumer groups or market segments or selected consumer groups, it is worthwhile for utilities to learn from elsewhere. Sketches of three options that were promoted by Durban Metro Water in selected unplanned areas are shown in Figure 2.4.

Book 2 of Serving all urban consumers examines 14 different water supply service options that have been used in different parts of the world. The potential advantages and disadvantages of the options from both the utility's and the consumers' point of view are also provided.

Payment options

Successful international water utility companies generally have a wide variety of payment options for their customers. This is essentially because they know that the easier they make it for customers to pay, the more likely those customers are to pay promptly. They know that people living in a city have a variety of different lifestyles and preferred payment methods. Severn Trent Water in the UK, for example, offers a number of payment options including:

• by post

- by direct debit

- at a bank

- at a building society

- at a post office

- at a payment point ('Paypoint') in a shop

- by home or telephone banking

- through the internet, via the utility's web-site

- by a Watercard.

Severn Trent Water have also found that not all customers are able to pay in the normal pattern of two payments per year. They have had to accept small payments on a monthly and even weekly basis to help those on low-incomes or social welfare benefits.

While a utility in a developing country may not offer quite the same list of options to its customers, they also have to think about suitable payment options for their high, medium and low-income customers. The method of payment is most important in urban areas of low-income countries where many households have a low disposable income.

Utilities serving low-income communities may wish to consider more flexible payment options, rather than monthly payments for individual connections. Utilities could negotiate with community groups or private individuals to manage water kiosks or shared connections, so that consumers pay the owners of the kiosk or shared connections small sums of money when they take water and the kiosk or shared connection owners pay the utility each month. Alternatively a utility could open customer offices in or near poor areas to enable more regular payments of water bills, such as weekly instalments.

Shared management options

It can be beneficial for a utility to share the management of water services with other partners such as community groups or vendor groups (small-scale water providers), particularly in low-income communities or areas that are poorly served. Such arrangements can reduce the utility's operational management costs and enable the vendors or community groups to be more effective in service provision.

Shared management with small water enterprises

There is potential for improved collaboration between the utility and small-scale providers or small water enterprises (SWEs), particularly in areas where the utility is unable to provide adequate services for some time. Alternatively, where the private vendors are charging high prices, which is very common, the utility can seek to capture more of the water market in those areas, by competing with vendors, and so increase customer satisfaction.

Shared management with community groups

Shared management of water services between a utility and local community groups can be cost efficient and can empower communities to manage their services and enable improved service provision in areas where a utility may be unable or reluctant to operate. For example, in Arusha, Tanzania and Dhaka, Bangladesh, community groups manage water kiosks that are supplied with water by the utility and payment is based on meter readings. Whereas in parts of Kibera (Nairobi), Haiti and Dakar (Senegal), community groups manage small tertiary water distribution systems and pay the utility or municipal council for the water supply on the basis of bulk meter readings.

Where a utility or municipality experiences difficulties in serving informal settlements; partnerships between a utility and community groups or with small water enterprises can be explored as a means of improving services. Intermediary organizations such as NGOs, consultants or university departments can contribute effectively to developing such partnerships, while the government departments concerned can encourage or create a supportive environment.

Partners for improved services to the poor

There are usually a number of stakeholders already working in slums or unplanned areas, such as local government, NGOs, CBOs, small water enterprises, etc. A key question for a utility is how could they best work with such organizations, taking advantage of their particular strengths, to improve services. Perhaps other organizations such as consultants could also contribute.

Utilities may consider setting up an inter-disciplinary team or an inter-departmental unit within the utility that can focus solely on services for informal settlements and liaison with other concerned stakeholders. Opportunities for collaboration with a variety of potential partners are discussed below. Opportunities for working with other stakeholders is best addressed as part of the process of deciding where to target efforts and resources.

Potential partners

Local authorities

Municipal officials often interact with local communities when dealing with a variety of services. In some cases municipal officers may have some responsibilities for improving sanitation or even water services in their area of jurisdiction. Local authorities will also usually have established structures for mobilising communities.

Local authorities may, in conjunction with the water utilities, also act as regulators of water vendors and other delegated enterprises, particularly if the municipality has a clear environmental health responsibility which relates to issues of water quality and sanitation. Municipalities dealing with the promotion of on-plot sanitation are also important partners for utilities who are contemplating extending service options such as sewerage and disposal facilities for suction trucks.

Small water enterprises or vendors

These are individual persons or groups who collect and sell water to households or other establishments in poorly served areas. Small water enterprises or small-scale providers have a number of positive aspects including those listed in Box 2.3.

Examples of the different types of small water enterprises (SWEs) or small-scale providers and the countries where they are used are listed in Table 2.4. Some SWEs are licensed while others are not.

It may be beneficial for the utility or municipality to assist in forming an association of SWEs in a city, or at least to collaborate with SWE groups, for the following reasons:

Box 2.3. Success factors of small-scale independent providers (SSIPs)[1]

Small service providers make a difference

Studies conducted in the four East African cities of Dar Es Salaam, Kampala, Mombasa and Nairobi in 1998 and 1999 listed the following success factors of small-scale independent providers (SSIP) in the water supply and sanitation services:

- Monopolistic public enterprises are often unable to respond to the dynamics of market demand.

- SSIP can access peri-urban areas not covered by the public enterprise.

- SSIP are commercially oriented.

- SSIP respond to the needs of the market by accessing high population density communities through the provision of standpipes and water kiosks.

- SSIP operate other business in addition to provision of urban environmental services.

1. Source: World Bank (2000)

Table 2.4. Examples of small water enterprises[1]

Type of small water enterprises	Examples of countries where used
Water trucks Sell water to distributing vendors or direct to consumers	Haiti, Mauritania, Tanzania and Uganda
Animal-drawn carts Vendors selling water to consumers or water carriers from donkey, camel or horse-pulled carts	Senegal, Mali, Mauritania
Water kiosk or standpipe vendors Engaged by utility, community or private owners to sell water to consumers	Kenya, Senegal, Uganda and Tanzania
Hand carts Selling water direct to consumers at or near their homes	Indonesia, Kenya, Vietnam, Burkina Faso
Water carriers by hand or cycles They sell water direct to consumers at or near their homes	Mali, Haiti, Uganda and India
Private boreholes May be connected to standpipes or house connections	Kenya and Mauritania
Small private pipe networks	Benin, Philippines, Guinea and Mali
On-selling to neighbours May be from yard taps or flexible pipe from neighbour's house	Kenya, Cote d'Ivoire, India, Uganda

1. Source: Derived from Collignon and Vezina (2000) and Lyonnaise des Eaux now Ondeo, Suez (1998)

- To share experiences about service provision in poorly served areas and how they may be improved.

- To provide a forum to consider how the utility could support SWEs in providing improved services, particularly where the utility is unable to serve for some time.

- To provide a forum for the utility/municipality to regulate the activities of SWEs in terms of price and quality of service.

Community-based organizations (CBOs)

To compensate for the limited capacities of municipalities and other public sector service providers in many low-income countries, civil society are forming community-based associations organized alongside various activities, such as micro-credit schemes, water and sanitation, health, church, youth, women's, or security neighbourhood associations. Many of these associations are interested in getting involved in determining the community's destiny in terms of major public services such as water, education, and health. CBOs can be effective partners in shared management arrangements for water services such as those discussed in the Kibera case study summarized in Box 2.4.

Box 2.4. Co-operative management of water distribution in Kibera, Nairobi

Kibera is one of the largest informal settlements in Africa, with a population of about 500,000 people and an estimated population density of 2,000 people per hectare. According to a survey conducted by the Water and Sanitation Program in Nairobi in Laini Saba, one of the nine villages in Kibera, the residents consider sanitation and water supply as the most crucial problems they face.

In response to the water supply problems in the area, Ushirika, a community-based organization in Laini Saba, created a partnership with a local NGO, Maji Ufanisi, to extend piped water services to the area. Maji Ufanisi provided materials and technical expertise, while the local community arranged for labour to lay the pipeline and construct the water kiosks. In collaboration with Nairobi City Council, a new distribution pipeline was extended to Laini Saba, which was commissioned in 1998.

A bulk flow meter was installed on the main distribution network where the Ushirika pipe connected and the Ushirika Co-operative Water Society are issued water bills on the basis of the bulk meter readings. A management committee was set up to manage the water project on behalf of Ushirika. Consumers pay for the water by volume at the new water kiosks. The tariff is higher than the bulk cost price charged by Nairobi City Council but less than other local vendors' prices. Ushirika hire staff to sell the water at 2 Kenyan shillings per jerrycan. These staff are paid a proportion of the money they collect according to the water meter at the kiosk. The surplus funds are then invested in other projects funded by Ushirika in Kibera

---

Water management committees

These committees are often set up during development projects to ensure sustainability through community management. The committee members could be elected by a ward council to manage water services in their area. These organizations can be useful partners if they are active and are considered reasonably representative of their community.

Non-government Organizations (NGOs) and university departments

The process of becoming involved with potential customers in their own environment in informal settlements involves skills, knowledge and experience that the utility may not have. This need not be a prohibiting factor as a number of options exist to bring such attributes in to the utility. For example, collaboration can be explored with local NGOs, civil society groups and social development specialists in universities. NGOs usually deal with a number of problems of concern to the community such as water, sanitation, income generation, solid waste management, etc. These organizations typically have good skills in facilitation, negotiation, and participatory planning which could be used by utilities intending to work in informal settlements.

Private consultancy companies

A wide range of consultancy companies are becoming more common in developing countries, and they are often able to offer expertise in working with community-based organiza-tions, fulfilling similar roles to NGOs. They may also be able to provide technical expertise. People who have gained experience with either NGOs or the public sector may move on to work as private consultants.

It would be beneficial for utilities and concerned government departments to consider the merits of either collaborating with or contracting such organizations to undertake defined roles in improving services in low-income areas. Further discussion of potential collabora-tions between utilities and government are included in Chapters 3 and 4.

Demand assessment - willingness-to-pay surveys

When it is proposed to improve services to parts of a utility's service area, viable service, payment and management options need to be developed after both learning lessons from elsewhere and consulting with key stakeholders. Demand assessment studies can then be carried out using methods such as willingness-to-pay surveys, where the user's maximum willingness to pay is determined for selected viable service options amongst each of the selected consumer groups or areas.

Determining which service options have clear demand and in which areas is a key part of the *targeting* process that leads to viable investment proposals.

Investment proposals in the water sector are best justified by using accurate demand assessment techniques such as willingness-to-pay surveys. There are various definitions of willingness to pay (WTP), but the most common one states that:

"WTP is the maximum amount that an individual states they are willing to pay for a good or service" (DFID Demand Assessment Seminar, December, 1997).

The urban water sector in low and middle-income countries (LMICs) require good quality data in order to:

• justify future investment proposals;

• develop a better understanding of user perceptions and preferences;

• support the selection of preferred service options; and

• set out the scope for future tariff increases and subsidy reduction plans.

Such information is vital for cost-effective sector development in the urban water sector. There are three main ways to estimate WTP:

a) Observe the prices that people are already paying for goods in various markets (i.e. water vending, buying from neighbours, paying local taxes).

b) Observe individual expenditures of money, time, labour, etc. to obtain goods - or to avoid their loss. This method might involve an assessment of coping strategies and involve observations, focus group discussions and even household surveys.

c) Asking people directly what they are willing to pay for goods or services in the future.

The first two approaches are based on observations of behaviour and are called Revealed Preference techniques. They can be very informative for studies on both vendor prices and on the coping costs and strategies of different consumer groups, and should be undertaken in each city/town in order to inform the scope for improvements by a utility.

The third technique (c) is based on stated preferences and includes the contingent valuation methodology (CVM). This technique is the most useful in that it determines the average *maximum willingness to pay* for different service options by each of the consumer groups where the options are viable. Book 2 provides examples of calculating coping costs for different consumer groups and information on conducting CVM surveys.

In order to ensure that sufficiently reliable data is obtained, use a robust contingent valuation survey methodology together with accurately priced and technically viable options. This will help to ensure that the results can be easily interpreted to produce useful design, implementation and policy recommendations. Offering between three and five options in the CVM survey is normally considered practical, although there are no firm rules (Wedgwood and Sansom, 2003).

An example of willingness-to-pay survey results for one market segment are shown in Tables 2.5. Note that both the weighted mean willingness-to-pay results and the 2/3 values given in these tables reveal a WTP that is much higher than the current tariff level in Mombasa in Kenya.

Table 2.5. WTP results for people in one to three-roomed dwellings in Mombasa[1]

Brief description of service option	Percentage of respondents within market segment who bid for the stated service option	Weighted mean WTP (KSh)	Amount which two-thirds of respondents are WTP (KSh)
1. Continuous supply at yard connection	100%	1124	834
2. Continuous supply with storage tank at shared yard connection	100%	1023	800
3. 12-hr supply at shared yard connection, rationing	62%	537	447
4. 4-Hr supply at shared yard connection	54%	395	336

1. Source: Njiru and Sansom, 2004
   (Exchange rate was KSh73 to US$1)

These results, along with the consumer survey information, can therefore be used to advocate for adequate tariff levels and flexible service options amongst key decision-makers. This information can then be used to determine an appropriate tariff policy and financing projection for the improved water supply services, often involving the allocation of appropriate subsidies for less convenient services.

Other techniques, such as the costed option ranking that is incorporated in the PREPP methodology described in Book 3 of *Serving all urban consumers*, can also be used to assess demand. The PREPP approach is particularly useful when working in informal settlements or for pilot projects that would not warrant the expense of a full WTP study.

2.6   Selling and providing services to low-income consumers

Once a utility has targeted areas where it wants to improve services, established partnerships with other stakeholders, and assessed demand for new options, it needs to consider how it can sell and provide service options on a sustainable basis, as part of the final step in the customer value chain. One useful marketing framework for developing appropriate strategies is the marketing mix.

The marketing mix

Bringing information from the consumer together with the ideas and expertise of the service provider is known as a 'marketing mix' (Wilson and Gilligan, 1998). This mix will be different from situation to situation, but will always contain elements of product, price, promotion, place, people, process and presence, or the *7Ps of marketing*.

A marketing mix is the means by which being demand responsive can become a reality. Development of a marketing mix involves creating a menu of service options that are based on reliable knowledge of the consumer's known preferences and an assessment of what the utility can realistically provide. Getting the marketing mix right involves the utility in a number of activities and areas of responsibility, such as those summarized in Figure 2.5.

The 'mix' in marketing is useful because, for example, the introduction of communal standposts with shared management *(product)* will not work without good communication (people). Decentralizing customer services to zone offices will not be effective without letting local customers know about the move *(promotion)*. The emphasis on *process* is also important.

The 7Ps is a simple marketing framework that can easily be used in workshops and meetings as a means of capturing the ideas of concerned staff and stakeholders. A more comprehensive approach for a utility to plan for a sustainable improvement in services to all consumer groups is the strategic marketing approach, which is outlined in Section 2.7

2.7   Pilot programmes in low-income areas and scaling up

For utilities who wish to use marketing approaches in low-income areas, it is advisable initially to develop pilot programmes in a few areas and learn lessons from those pilots. It is also important to demonstrate that it is possible to serve the poor effectively on a pilot basis in the city or town in question, before considering an integrated methodology for city-wide and long-term scaling up using the necessary strategic planning.

| Product | • Offer options menu (including technology, service level, price, management arrangements, payment choices, etc., based on consumer preferences and utility ability to deliver) |

| Price | • Tariff structure
• Discounts for shared management schemes
• Profitability
• Competitiveness
• Price incentives
• Willingness and ability to sustain payment |

| Promotion | • Advertising (paper-based, loudspeaker, radio, press releases)
• Word-of-mouth (through front office and field staff; other customers)
• Community meetings, focus groups
• Sales promotion e.g. new service option demonstrations
• Public relations |

| Place | • Market segmentation plan
• Ability to supply target group
• Local external influences and/or political dynamics
• Local competitive advantage
• Local logistical support (decentralized O&M, payment schemes and customer services)
• Different products in different market segments |

| People | • Quality of customer relationship
• Two-way communication structures and mechanisms
• Development of trust
• Understanding perceptions and expectations
• Loyalty to existing / potential service provider
• Customer feedback
• Human resources development / capacity building
• Liaison and partnerships with civil society, NGOs, donors |

| Process | • Complaint/compliments monitoring systems
• Quality control for technical and billing systems
• Service delivery reliability and consistency
• Streamlined service procedures (connections, customer inquiries, re-connection, service recovery systems) |

| Presence | • Premises (decentralized/centralized)
• Accessibility of utility to customers
• Customer service office (location, atmosphere, image, accessibility, ease of use)
• Local liaison teams / officers
• Corporate image; corporate identity |

Figure 2.5. Water utility marketing mix issues[1]

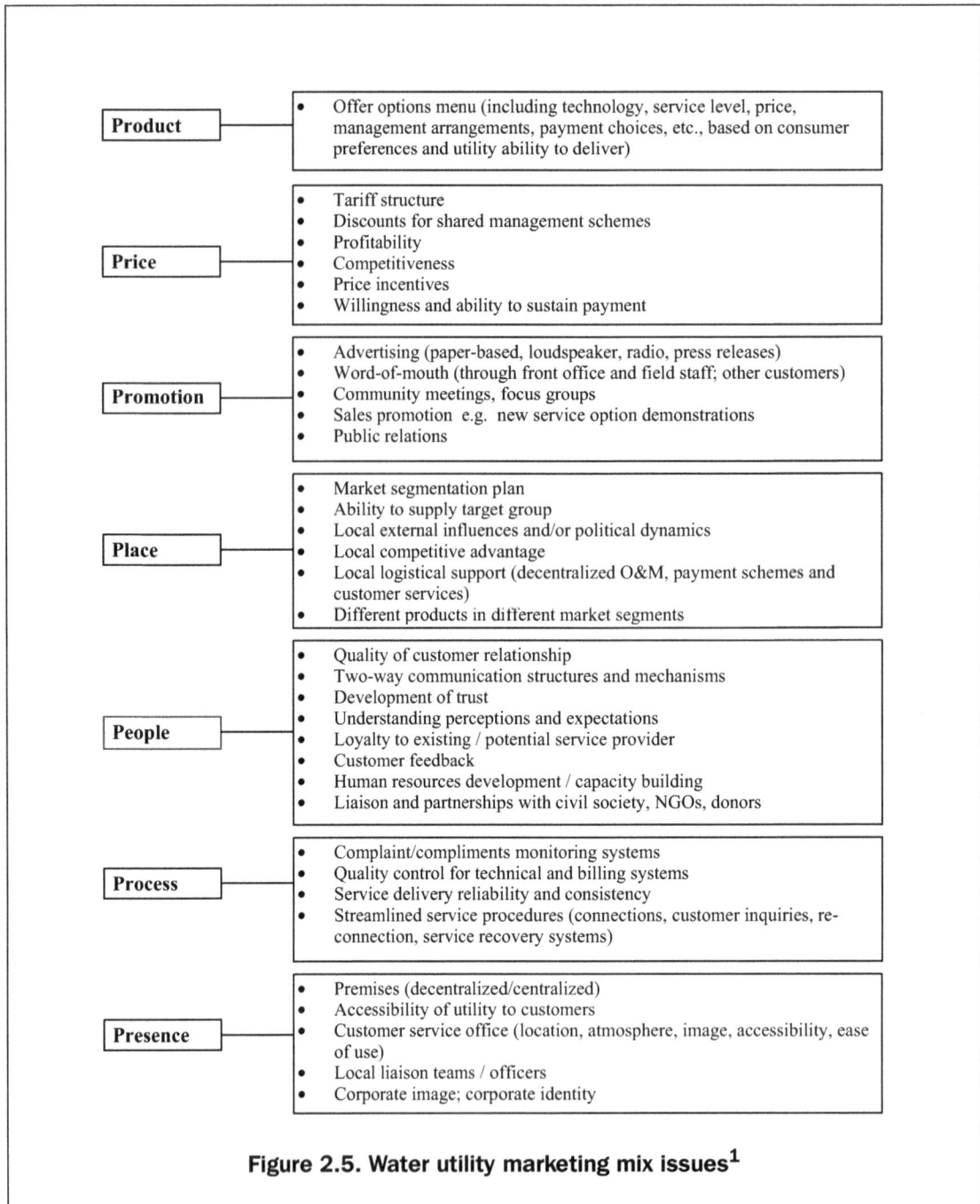

1. Adapted from: Brassington and Pettitt, (2000)

Serving the poor is made more possible in the average utility because of the availability of 'surplus water' that is lost through leakage, illegal connections and other means. Water saved through activities such as leak reduction programmes can be directed towards immediate service improvement to the poor. There does not usually have to be any parallel delivery of new water sources and treatment in order to demonstrate the viability of delivery to informal areas because of the extent of non-revenue water, which can be as high as 50-60 per cent. Indeed, the apparent reason for one water utility to serve the unplanned areas around their city was the embarrassment of surplus water achieved through a leakage reduction programme. They needed to do something with it and recognized the ready market on their doorstep (Nickson, 2001).

When selecting pilot areas, it is worthwhile choosing communities where there is a clear demand for improved services and where there are community groups who are willing to collaborate in developing appropriate service, payment and management options. Capable intermediaries such as NGOs or consultants can assist in developing and maintaining effective dialogue with community groups. For the initial pilot projects it is preferable to work in areas where there are good prospects for success so that partners can learn what works best before taking on more difficult areas.

When scaling up to city-wide approaches, it is beneficial to gather information about the experiences, perceptions and preferences of *all* consumer groups. This enables a utility to develop valuable comparative data to prioritize its investments and resources, as well developing appropriate and specific marketing strategies for each consumer group.

Scaling up to meet the needs of a larger city or town entails balancing price and service differentiation between the various consumer groups. This necessitates a 'Strategic Marketing' approach as part of city-wide planning . These aspects are discussed in the next section.

2.8   The strategic marketing framework

The examples given so far indicate how the demand/responsive marketing approach can be used to pilot water (and possibly sanitation) services to low-income consumers by using innovative and participatory ways of working. To ensure that this type of approach can be replicated across all low-income areas in a city with long-term sustainability ensured, a strategic marketing approach is required. What can be made to work with special effort in a few low-income areas in a city can have a different impact on a utility's operations when it has to be scaled up across the entire city, particularly when up to 60 per cent of the population may be living in informal low-income housing areas.

There are a number of reasons why, after initial piloting work, marketing plans for urban water services needs to be reasonably strategic and comprehensive, including the following:

- Utilities need to feel confident that if they offer new options and services, then they can provide them on a sustainable and reliable basis. Comprehensive investment and strategic marketing planning can contribute to increasing this level of confidence, particularly when potential financiers agree to fund agreed investment plans.

- Precedence and equity are also important considerations. If one slum area has new service options, there will eventually be a lot of pressure to serve other slums in a similar way, so broader strategic planning is required.

- The proportion of urban residents living in informal settlements or unplanned areas is growing, hence the need to address the perception, needs and preferences of this important group in utility-wide investment planning and institutional development.

Strategic marketing is a comprehensive approach for organizations to make the case for investment through understanding the perceptions and preferences of different customer groups and their willingness to pay for different types of services. This leads to the development of viable business plans for targeting and promoting appropriate service, payment and management options that can be provided reliably to each of those customer groups or market segments at appropriate prices.

Stage 1:
Where are we now?

Develop suitable criteria for market segmentation then assess the following for the utility and each market segment/ area:
a) Key stakeholder roles and perceptions
b) Consumer perceptions and experiences
c) Initial demands for improved services
d) Current service levels amongst all consumer groups
e) Performance against key indicators, targets and objectives
f) Water and sewerage infrastructure deficiencies and condition of assets
g) Water resources availability and environmental issues
h) Utility staff perceptions and capabilities
i) The utility/municipal finances
j) Alternative water service providers
k) Key Institutional problems, including barriers to serving the poor and possible solutions

Stage 2
Where do we want to be?

For each market segment/area:
a) Consider the 'where are we now' information and review organizational objectives, targets and priorities
b) If there is clear demand/need for service improvements, then develop service options, technical designs and cost estimates.
c) Undertake detailed demand assessment (e.g. WTP surveys)
d) Estimate population projections and take-up of service options
e) Agree revised performance targets in each area
f) Agree proposed infrastructure improvements
g) Agree operations plans for preferred options
h) Agree what options in terms of services, payment and shared management are feasible at what tariff levels for different areas?
i) Prepare financial projections of projected costs and revenues, including proposed tariff levels

Figure 2.6. Strategic marketing activities for improving water services (Part A)

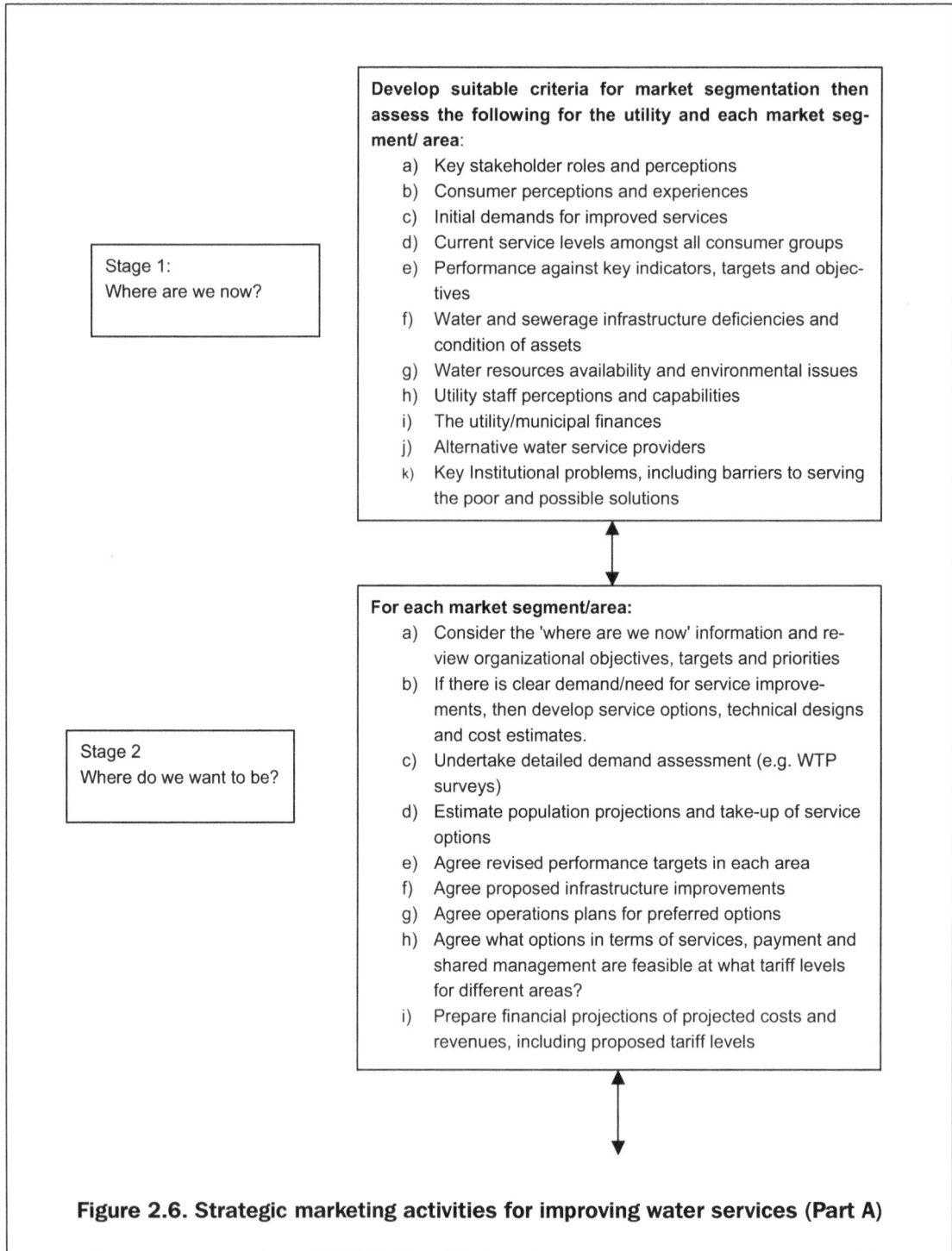

A strategic marketing methodology developed by Wilson and Gilligan (1997) has been used and adapted in these publications as part of the research programme in Africa and India. During the research, Strategic Marketing Plans (SMPs) for Water Services were developed to test the methodology in a number of cities and towns around the world including Mombasa, Kampala and Lesotho in Africa and Guntur, Agra and various small towns in Nepal in South Asia. Three of these SMPs are available on the WEDC web-site at: www.lboro.ac.uk/wedc/projects/psd/.

Typical key activities involved in the strategic marketing process for urban water services are set out in Figure 2.6 and Figure 2.7. The main stages ask the questions:

Stage 3
How might we get there?

For each market segment/area:
a) Consider utility 'product positioning' (compared to alternative providers such as vendors and private borewells)
b) Develop a marketing strategy using the 'marketing mix' (7Ps), including a promotion plan.
c) Consider how to support preferred service and payment options
d) Consider how to support proposed shared management arrangements either with small-scale providers or community groups
e) Develop an institutional improvements plan, considering PPP options
f) Develop a 'customer relations management' strategy
g) Evaluate benefits and risks
h) Summarize Stages 1, 2 and 3 in an Investment or Strategic Marketing Plan (SMP) or business plan and consult key stakeholders
i) Seek appropriate sources of funding.

Stage 4:
How can we ensure success?

Implement and revise the Strategic Marketing or Investment Plans considering good practice such as:
a) Institutional development and sector reform
b) Use of appropriate PPP options and regulation
c) Well-designed participatory change management approaches
d) Total Quality Management (TQM) approaches
e) Monitoring and evaluation

Figure 2.7. Strategic marketing activities for improving water services (Part B)

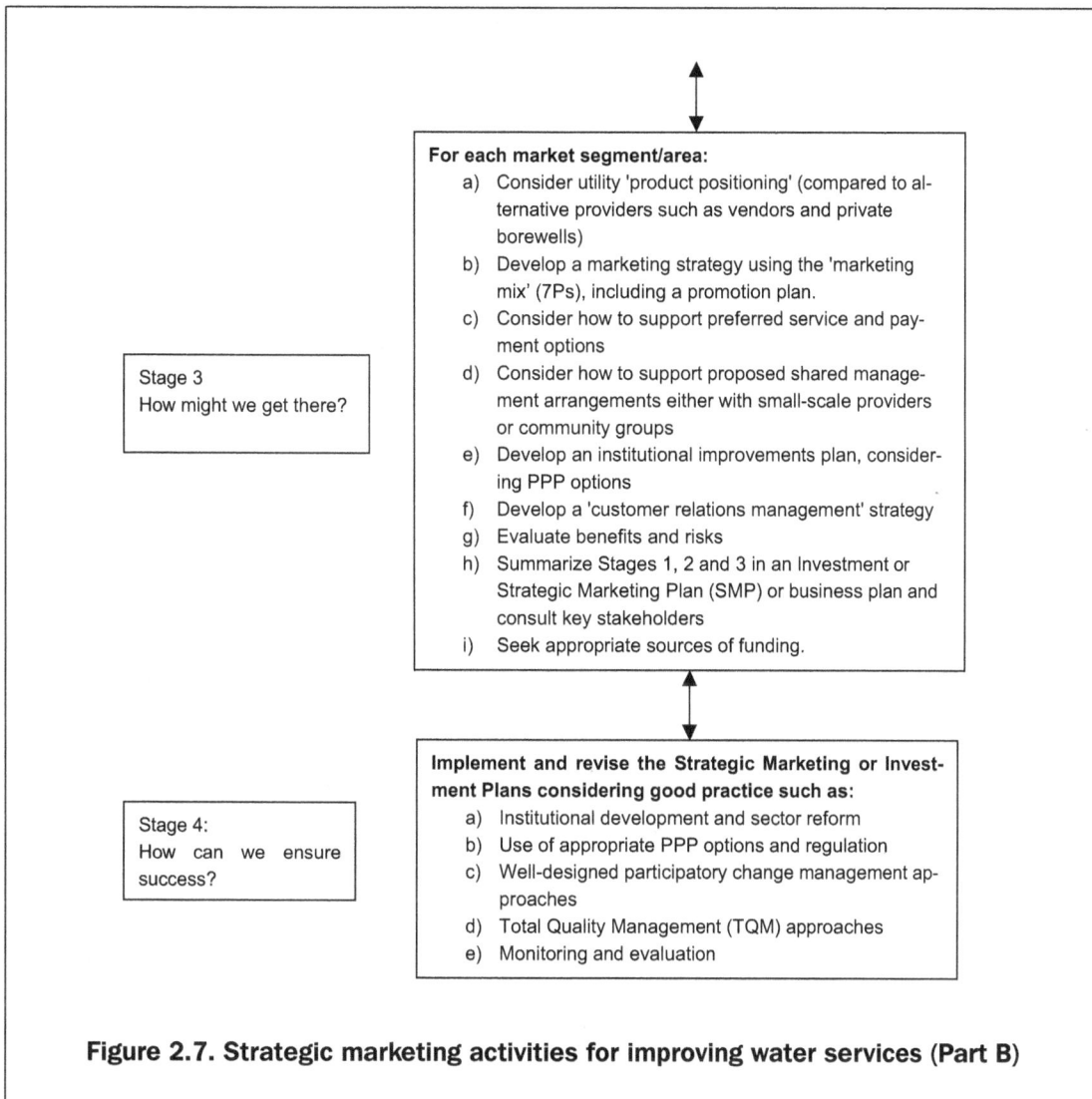

- *Where are we now?*
- *Where do we want to be?*
- *How might we get there?*
- *How do we ensure success?*

Note that there are double arrows between each stage in the figures, which emphasizes that these are iterative processes where it may be necessary to go back one or two stages at certain times. These four questions can form a natural structure for an SMP report. However, a utility needs to be mindful of the preferred report formats of potential financiers.

This publication, and the urban water sector research that formed the foundation for it, focus more on the first three (planning) stages. For guidance on dealing with stage four (How do we ensure success?) we recommend publications on marketing, Public Private Partnerships, institutional development and change management, Total Quality Management (TQM), and other conventional business manuals.

It may be tempting for utility managers to complete each of the four stages of strategic marketing in very broad terms. For example at the end of the 'where do we want to be?' stage, if the final output is just a statement of the utility's objectives, then the strategic marketing plan and process will be of limited benefit.

This exercise is much more useful if at the end of the 'where do we want to be' phase there are detailed utility financial projections of future costs and revenues, based on a thorough analysis of the factors listed in Stage 1, for all consumer groups. This is a key finding of research in Africa and India conducted by the research partners involved in this publication.

Typical strategic marketing outputs

Some of the key outputs that can be produced at each stage as part of an effective strategic marketing process typically include:

Stage 1: Where are we now? Utility situation assessment report(s) with comprehensive documentation and analysis of aspects listed in Figure 2.6, such as: service levels, perceptions of all consumer groups, utility performance, alternative service providers, institutional issues and barriers to serving the poor, etc., provide a good basis for proceeding to Stage 2.

Stage 2: Where do we want to be? Suggested outputs from this stage, assuming an investment plan for service improvement is being developed for the different consumer groups, are:

- outline design options and proposals;

- a detailed demand assessment (e.g. WTP survey report) for target areas;

- proposed service/payment and management options to be offered for each market segment or area;

- a review of utility objectives, targets and priorities; and

- financial projections of cost and revenues as part of an investment plan, including different investment scenarios. The preferred financial plans need to be both realistic and affordable.

Stage 3: How might we get there? Outputs could include: a review of the proposed investment options or scenarios, and an institutional development report that may include PPP options and a strategic marketing or investment plan for potential financiers and other key stakeholders.

The outputs from Stage 4 *(How do we ensure success?)* will be the successful implementation of activities that have been planned in Stages 2 and 3, making any required changes to the plans in the light of experience.

It is important that an element of realism is used in the planning process, as unrealistic plans tend to get ignored. In addition, it is beneficial to involve as many staff and key stakeholders in the planning process as is feasible, and in a participatory manner, as this is likely to lead to better commitment at the implementation stage. Developing a shared understanding and agreement about the plans being developed can be done through small group consultations, meetings and workshops.

The overall extent to which the organization is commercially and customer-orientated will have a significant impact on the successful implementation of a marketing strategy. In the context of the water sector in developing countries, the strategic marketing plan (SMP) is a framework for the sustainable improvement of water services and mainstreaming of poverty reduction in the utility's business. A good strategic marketing plan (SMP) shows how the utility can improve services to customers and potential customers and at the same time be financially sustainable.

The three stages of strategic marketing planning are briefly considered in the following sections. More detailed guidance on completing these stages is contained in *Book 2* for managers.

2.9   Stage 1: Where are we now?

It is important for an organization to objectively establish its current position. Information on 'Where are we now?' can be obtained by carrying out institutional analysis of the utility, including an assessment of the utility's existing water-supply infrastructure and services.

High-quality consumer surveys provide useful information on the water market, such as the perceptions and preferences of existing and potential customers for improvements in services. Such consumer data provides a good starting point for developing the analysis of the utility's performance and opportunities for improvement.

Reliable data compared against key indicators forms the basis of effective performance measurement, which is important to utilities and to government departments as well in their role as creators of enabling environments and as regulators. Section 3.6 in the next chapter provides a summary of the benefits and main steps entailed in performance measurement.

A comprehensive assessment of where the utility is now using a variety of survey and appraisal techniques is required so that adequate plans can be developed for improved and more reliable services to all consumer groups.

Tools such as PEST analysis (political, environmental, social and technological) and SWOT analysis (strengths, weaknesses, opportunities and threats) are very useful in understanding an institution and its environment, and these are discussed further in *Book 2*. The analysis should also include progress on reform issues and services to the poor. A SWOT analysis is a good way of summarizing all the quantitative and qualitative information collected to help the utility answer the question 'where are we now?'.

Typical urban water indicators
Performance should be assessed in terms of trends over a number of years, rather than snapshots of performance. The most common performance indicators for water supply utilities relate to the dimensions of production, delivery, consumption, efficiency, effectiveness and finance. It is important to note that no single indicator is sufficient to provide a meaningful picture.

Table 2.6 shows examples of finance and economic indicators and ratios that are important for a utility's financial health. Table 2.7 shows typical key performance indicators and ratios that could be adapted for a given utility. Note that there are columns in the tables for recording actual values and target values. This is a useful means of planning improvements and monitoring progress. When assessing utility finances it is important to examine both hidden and apparent subsidies.

Table 2.6. Financial indicator and ratio examples

Category	Indicator or ratio	Formulae	Previous years value	Latest actual value	Target for next year
Marketing	Socio-economic GNP per capita				
	Average WTP to 'vendors				
Financial sustainability	Average domestic tariff				
	Community standpost tariff				
	Sewerage tariff				
Profitability	Operating ratio	$\frac{\text{total cost}}{\text{total revenue}}$			
	Return on fixed assets	$\frac{\text{profit after depreciation}}{\text{net fixed assets}}$			
Liquidity	Current ratio	$\frac{\text{current assets}}{\text{current liabilities}}$			
Credit-worthiness	Debt:equity ratio	$\frac{\text{Long-term loans}}{\text{equity}}$			
Financial efficiency	Days receivable ratio	$\frac{365 \times \text{accounts receivable}}{\text{annual billed revenue}}$			
	Bill collection efficiency	% of bills collected			

Those utilities who are considering a benchmarking programme, should refer to the World Bank benchmarking toolkit for water and sanitation on their website. It is also beneficial to collect data per market segment or area, so that priority areas for improvement amongst each consumer group can be identified. A sample format for indicators and ratios by market segment, particularly for serving low-income areas, is given in Section 3.6.

Where possible the data based on these indicators can be from utility databases or collected using regular well-designed consumer surveys that are representative of each market segment or consumer group. This process also enables ongoing effective monitoring against agreed targets in conjunction with the regulator or appropriate government department.

Table 2.7. Financial indicator and ratio examples

Category	Indicator or ratio	Formulae	Previous years value	Latest actual value	Target for next year
Water production	Quantity of water produced	Volume treated/per target population			
	Quality of water produced	Percentage samples acceptable			
	Production factor	Energy and chemicals costs as percentage of operating costs			
Water delivery (for whole city)	Target population				
	Average no. of people/ connection	Total population/no. of connections			
	Standpipe use	Percentage of population who use standpipes or kiosks			
	Service delivery (use)	Percentage of people who use house or yard connections			
	Supply hours	Average supply hours per day at acceptable pressure			
Efficiency	Unaccounted for water	Percentage of water paid for/water produced			
	Maintenance efficiency	Frequency of burst/km pipes			
	Maintenance efficiency	Average downtime of electromechanical plant			
	Maintenance spending	Percentage maintenance expenditure of total operating expenses			
Consumption	Quantity of water consumed per person	Served population/water consumed			
	Working meters	Percentage of working consumption meters			
	Quality of water delivered	Percentage samples acceptable			
Sewerage	Service coverage	Percentage population connected to sewers			
		Percentage population with acceptable on-site sanitation			
	Maintenance	Frequency of failure/km sewers			
	Treatment	Percentage of wastewater treated			
Effectiveness	Extent of water related diseases	Diarrhoea /cholera/ typhoid cases per million per year			
	Customer satisfaction surveys	Proportion customers questioned expressing satisfaction			
Productivity	Staffing levels	Staff per thousand connections			
		Staffing costs as percentage of operating costs			

2.10   Stage 2: Where do we want to be?

The completion of a thorough situation analysis (Stage 1) of the utility, and its' services, consumer groups and working environment, provides a good basis for beginning to answer the question *Where do we want to be?* It is necessary to review and agree utility objectives and targets in the light of information collected at the *Where are we now stage*.

Specific objectives need to be considered for different parts of the services provided. For example, specific and realistic targets are required for water and sanitation as well as for the different segments of the customer base, as a basis for investment planning.

Viable service options need to be selected, for each market segment, at appropriate prices. Part of the process of selecting feasible options and determining tariffs is to ensure that the views of customers have been taken into account, whether through customer committees, or information derived from customer surveys and willingness-to-pay studies. Verification of demand assessment data can be very useful. For example, using WTP or PREPP results as a basis for discussions with community groups or customer committees can increase the level of support for new proposals.

Projections of costs for improvements and the revenues that the utility can obtain should also be carefully made. In particular, the projections should show how the utility can improve water services to existing and potential customers and achieve financial sustainability. Estimates for option take-up will therefore need to be made, and spreadsheet calculations undertaken to project future revenues. An example of a financial projections summary sheet for a strategic marketing plan from Kampala can be seen in Annex 1.

As the ultimate aim in the process is to develop viable and comprehensive investment or strategic marketing plans, it is useful to think about a typical investment planning process and the inter-linkages between the various key activities and at what stages the key sets of information are used. An outline process showing these inter-linkages is shown in Figure 2.8. The process begins with Box 1: an assessment of current service levels and operations which should reveal key problems and any need for service improvements. It is also important to regularly conduct consumer surveys (Box 2) to find out consumers' (existing and potential customers) perceptions about both the service provision and the utility. Activities in Boxes 1 to 3 help answer the question *Where are we now?*

The key stage in the *Where we want to be?* section of the flowchart in Figure 2.8 is Box 4: 'Review objectives, targets, priorities and investment plans'. This should be done with the best available information, such as the data from the 'assessment of current service levels and operations (Box 1) and well-designed consumer surveys (Box 2), as well as the issues in Box 3.

If significant new or revised investments are proposed, then it is worthwhile developing 'service options, outline technical designs and cost estimates' (Box 5) and conducting 'Demand assessment e.g. willingness-to-pay surveys' (Box 6). Both these activities provide valuable information for developing the 'Financial projections including proposed tariffs' - Box 8, as well as the 'operations plans for preferred options' - Box 7. The willingness-to-pay survey results not only provide useful data on consumer preferences, but also the average maximum willingness-to-pay data is valuable in

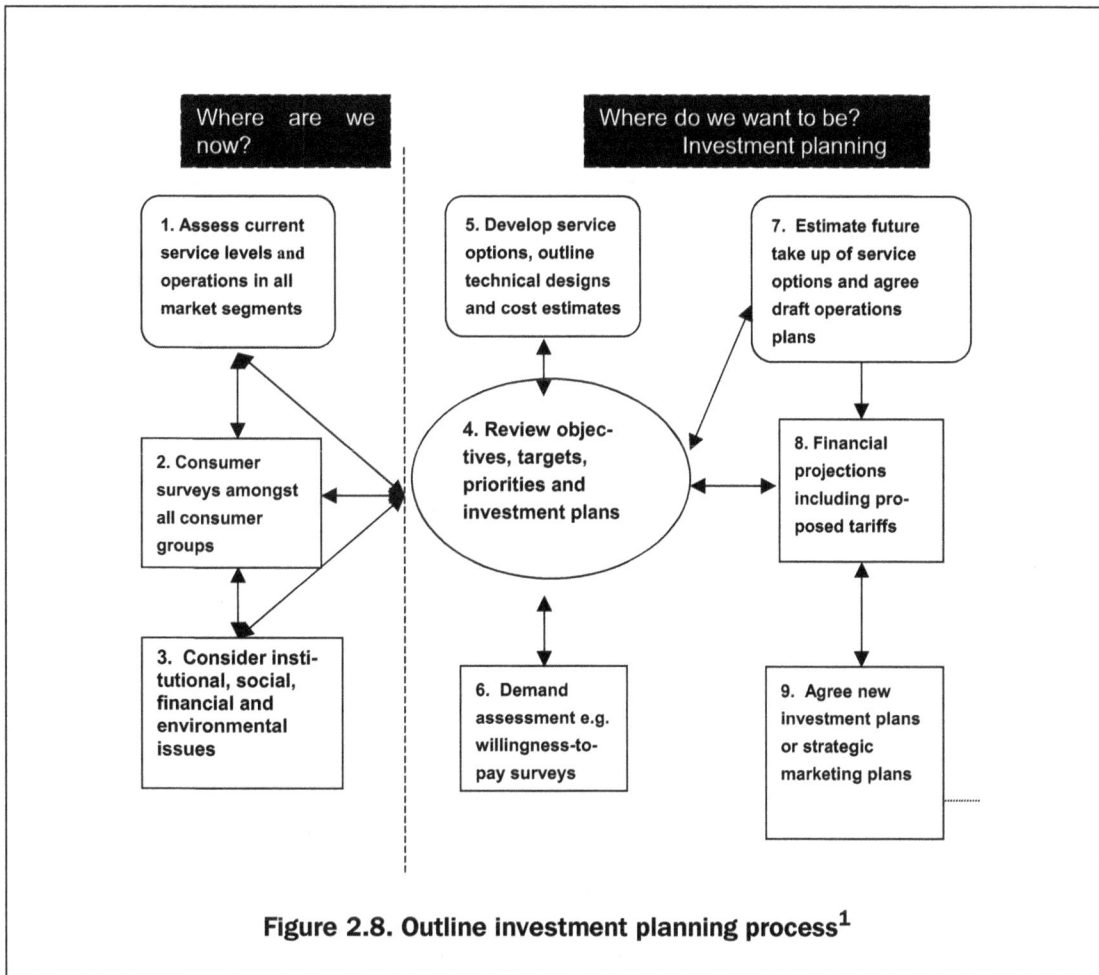

Figure 2.8. Outline investment planning process[1]

1. Source: K. Sansom adapted from Revels (2002)

determining tariff policies. Note that many of the arrows in the outline investment planning process figure point in both directions. This emphasizes that the process is both iterative and ongoing.

Potential infrastructure development may include bulk water supply, treatment, transmission and distribution to meet both current and future needs. Key areas for improvement are likely to be customer services such as billing, revenue collection, general customer relations and services to low-income areas. These 'software' issues ought to go hand-in-hand with 'hardware' issues such as infrastructure improvements and O&M that together constitute service quality. Improvements in service quality can result in the enhancement of customers' perception of the value of the service. Customers are often willing to pay more for a perceived increase in service quality, so the scope for increasing water tariffs increases.

The financial projections are best done using a number of investment scenarios. Refer to Box 2.5 for discussion of investment scenarios used for a draft Strategic Marketing Plan for Kampala. The preferred investment scenario can then form the basis of the agreed investment plan, which needs to be discussed with key stakeholders. A sample investment plan that was developed as part of a strategic marketing plan is shown in Annexe 2.

Box 2.5. Example financial projections for investments in Kampala[1]

During the dictatorial regime in Uganda in 1970-80 the service coverage of the corporatized urban water utility, National Water & Sewerage Corporation (NWSC), suffered in two major ways: there was virtually no investment into expanding water service coverage, and the existing infrastructure deteriorated because of poor O&M practices. Consequently, since 1986, NWSC has injected substantial investment funds into its infrastructure, using grants and loans sourced by the government from bilateral and multi-lateral financing institutions, with a loan repayment period ranging between 10 years and 30 years. Since the early 1990s, the loan portfolio for Kampala water supply service area has accumulated to about US$64 million.

Scrutiny of the investments carried out shows that expansion of water treatment plant was not matched by extension and rehabilitation of NWSC's water reticulation network, a situation that has resulted into a low service coverage of about 40 per cent of the total population in Kampala. On top of the high un-accounted-for-water and low collection efficiency, the low coverage contributed low revenue collection. Subsequently, NWSC asked for a reschedule of loan repayments as follows:

US$7.5 million in 2002/2003
US$8.3 million in 2003/2004
US$8.8 million in 2004/2005, leaving a principal balance of US$14.45 million on the historical loans.

Analysis carried out shows that it is not possible to both conform with this loan repayment schedule and use internal sources to capitalize the infrastructure expansion projects that are critical for the growth of NWSC. Consequently, to illustrate how to derive a 25-year strategic marketing plan for NWSC Kampala supply area, four scenarios were considered:

* *Scenario 1:* Assumptions were made that the central government will take on payment of historical loans, and treat it as equity contribution. In this case, revenue collection would fully cater for operation and maintenance costs, as well as service expansion to cover 100 per cent of projected population by year 25 of the project. The average tariff would be US$0.67 per cubic metre.

* *Scenario 2:* Assumptions were that revenue collection would cater for historical loans and service expansion to enable 100 per cent population coverage by year 25 of the project cycle. However, NWSC would have to negotiate for loan rescheduling to the last 10 years of the 25-year project cycle. The average tariff would be US$0.76 per cubic metre.

* *Scenario 3:* Assumptions were that the Central Government will take on payment of historical loans, and revenue collection would cater for service expansion to enable 100 per cent population coverage by year 25t of the project cycle. Kampala Area could also provide cross-subsidies of US$8 million in the first six years and step it up appropriately thereafter to cater for operation and maintenance of other secondary towns under NWSC. The average tariff would be US$0.76 per cubic metre.

* *Scenario 4:* Revenue collection to cater for both historical loan repayment and subsidies specified in Scenario 3. The major assumption is that NWSC would negotiate for rescheduling of loan repayment to after year 15 of the project, to enable capitalization of service expansion in the early period of the project. The tariff would be US$0.78 per cubic metre.

All the above scenarios ensured that there are no cash-flow problems in the daily operations of NWSC.

1. Source: Kayaga and Sansom (2003)

The potential revenues are compared with projected costs for each investment scenario to check for financial sustainability. This is an iterative activity that may have to be done several times until an acceptable combination of service options, costs and prices is achieved, each time keeping in mind customer's requirements and willingness to pay. When an acceptable combination is achieved, the utility should then move to the next stage of 'How might we get there?'. There may of course be more than one viable investment scenario in the financial projections, all of which might require further assessment.

The goal of financial sustainability, a return on capital employed, will place a heavy burden on customers who may have been used to receiving subsidized water (though it may deliver a dramatic reduction in prices to the poorest who have been purchasing water from vendors). This higher price burden is only fair if the water utility also bears its share through delivering services in the most efficient manner. 'Where do we want to be?' must also be answered in terms of a 'least-cost provider'.

2.11 Stage 3: How might the water utility get there?

The financial projections for new investment programmes and the most viable investment scenarios developed need to be assessed, after consideration of marketing and institutional issues, in order to develop the final strategic marketing plan, or investment plan.

The development of a viable marketing strategy, perhaps using the 7Ps (product, price, promotion, place, people, process and presence) is important, as are the development of institutional development proposals, including any public-private partnership options. It is also advisable to assess the potential risks and benefits of the preferred SMP.

Full consultation of the preferred strategic marketing plan among key stakeholders will assist in achieving a realistic plan and will help gain commitment. Negotiations with potential financiers are advisable, whether they be donors, banks or private operators seeking PPP arrangements. This is particularly important during the *'How might we get there?'* stage, so that project proposals can be prepared in the preferred format of interested funding organizations.

More information on how a water utility can successfully implement its strategic marketing or investment plans is provided in Chapter 8 of Book 2. Potential initiatives for governments to support these approaches are discussed in Section 3.2 and Chapter 4 of this book.

Chapter 3

Incentives for serving the urban poor

3.1   Introduction and overview

Achieving the right balance of incentives and penalties for utility service provision in order to achieve objectives such as effectiveness, efficiency and equity, is a major challenge for any government. Implementing penalties for organisations in a fair manner can be difficult, requiring comprehensive regulation. It is for this reason that we focus on incentives or incentive mechanisms in this publication. In many cases providing the right incentives can be sufficient motivation for organisations and individuals to improve performance as part of a change process.

Incentives can take many forms; this chapter discusses some of the policy-level incentives governments can usefully provide for urban water utilities and other stakeholders, as well as incentives utilities can provide to other stakeholders and directly to poor consumers.

Potential policy level initiatives

A number of government policy initiatives that can potentially create the right incentive mechanisms and enabling environment for sector stakeholders are outlined in section 3.3. The guiding principles behind such initiatives include the need to improve accountability of service providers for improving services to all consumer groups, through initiatives such as performance agreements. If the accountability of service providers to achieve agreed targets is increased, then those service providers need to be empowered to achieve the agreed objectives. An important step in empowering utilities is to give them sufficient financial and organisational autonomy so that they have the flexibility and capability to achieve targets.

Another key guiding principle is to improve the transparency in the way utilities, government and regulators make decisions and operate. Effective performance measurement arrangements are important for promoting improved transparency. A variety of consumer survey techniques should be used to produce reliable data against key indicators. Survey results need to be cross-checked with the utility's own data. It should be possible to disaggregate data for individual low-income areas in order to properly plan, monitor and evaluate service improvements.

Potential utility initiatives and incentives for serving the poor

A number of detailed initiatives that a utility could develop to provide better incentives for consumers in low income areas to become satisfied customers who pay their water bills are outlined in section 3.4. Such initiatives involve the utility in becoming more innovative and flexible in overcoming barriers (such as land tenure issues) in order to adequately serve informal settlements. A useful broad aim is to make it easier for consumers to be-come reliable paying customers, and to encourage preferred alternative service and payment options for those consumers who cannot afford their own connections, such as in-creasing the on-selling of good quality water.

Initiatives and incentives for working with CBOs, NGOs and SWEs

In the low income areas of most cities and towns CBOs, NGOs and small water enterprises operate to varying degrees doing useful work in providing or supporting services either together with utilities or on their own. Some key questions for utilities, governments and regulators include:

- What work do these stakeholders currently undertake and what comparative advantage do they have to undertake these tasks?

- How could each of these groups be supported to enhance their current performance?

- How could such stakeholders assist utilities in improving services to low income areas?

New initiatives and incentives are likely to be necessary if the last two questions above are to be addressed. Utilities may often be reluctant to engage constructively with NGOs, CBOs and SWEs because they are too busy in day to day operations or because they have different perspectives. It is for this reason that an important role for government and regu-lators is to facilitate collaboration or partnership between utilities and other stakeholders. This may entail the government taking a leading role at the beginning of the process. In the longer term the objective would be for utilities to actively seek to collaborate better with such stakeholders. Typical facilitator roles for government are outlined in section 4.1.

In conclusion, the main role for government and regulators is to ensure that:

a) It provides appropriate incentive mechanisms and an enabling environment for utilities to serve the poor effectively, and

b) It encourages utilities to provide better incentives for CBOs, NGOs and small water enterprises, so that they can contribute more effectively in improving services.

3.2   The need for incentives to serve poor communities

Field studies show that urban water utilities in many low-income countries have not been able to extend services to low-income communities. Often, water and sanitation services in the urban centres are available to high and middle-income earners only. Box 3.1 shows an example of service disparity in a city in a low-income country.

A similar situation occurs in other Africa cities where 75 per cent of the urban poor receive at least some of their water from small-scale providers, usually at very high prices. In India only about 42 per cent of urban dwellers have access to tap water in their premises. Urban water utilities in low-income countries advance several reasons for not servicing low-income communities effectively. Some of these reasons are:

Box 3.1. Water and sanitation service coverage in Kampala City[1]

Kampala, the capital city of Uganda, has a daytime population of about 1.2 million people. National Water and Sewerage Corporation (NWSC) is the sole provider of piped water and sewerage services. As of 1997:

- Over 50 per cent of Kampala residents lived below the government-designated poverty line of less than US$1 per capita per day, and live in low-income, unplanned settlements.
- Only 42 per cent of the residents were served with piped water supply.
- There were virtually no house connections in low-income settlements.
- Only 5 per cent of residents of low-income settlements received water through public standpipes.
- Of the 9 per cent of the residents who had access to the central sewerage system, only two-thirds were connected, while the rest of the people living in planned areas relied on septic tanks for wastewater disposal.

The rest of the residents relied on pit latrines for their waste disposal.

---

1. Source: Collignon and Vezina (2000)

- Low revenue collection results in little or no provision for infrastructure development to new areas.

- Poor infrastructure in the low-income settlements, i.e. not well planned, no roads, etc. means utilities find it difficult to extend services.

- The complex land tenure system impedes extension of conventional water and sanitation structures and systems.

- The initial capital costs for water and sewerage connections are high, and residents of low-income communities may not be able to afford them.

- Perception (on the side of the utility) that people in low-income settlements cannot afford to pay for services.

- Inadequate capacity on the part of the utility to serve low-income communities, i.e. no provision in the utility for specialized staff to handle such issues.

- Unclear responsibilities for working in informal settlements.

In order to accelerate service provision to low-income communities in urban centres, governments need to create incentives for the urban utilities and other stakeholders to overcome such barriers where it is feasible.

3.3   Potential policy-level initiatives

In order to improve water services in low-income communities, there is a need to have institutional and technical innovations at different levels. A key to encouraging innovations, partnerships and positive action on the ground is to create the right incentives and policies for the key stakeholders. These can be provided by both government and utilities.

At the policymaking level, there should be incentives, disincentives and supporting pro-poor policies. Examples of incentive mechanisms and supportive policies include:

- clear government policies promoting 'universal service obligations' as a primary duty and setting yearly targets for service improvements to all consumer groups, which will form the basis of monitoring progress;

- performance agreements between governments or regulators and the utilities that incorporate service improvements against agreed targets in a financially sustainable manner;

- revised mission statements that reflect improved services to all consumer groups in a financially sustainable manner;

- well designed performance measurement arrangements that use a variety of consumer survey techniques producing reliable data against key indicators. It should be possible to disaggregate data for individual low-income areas in order to properly plan, monitor and evaluate service improvements.

- benchmarking programmes using appropriate indicators, that enable fair comparisons between utilities;

- more flexibility on human resource management issues such as appointments and staff remuneration;

- more flexible service provision standards or norms that allow more innovative service options that specifically meet the needs of low income areas at affordable prices.

- appropriate use of private operators (national and international) with PPP contracts that have incentives for serving the poor;

- ensuring that small water enterprises and community based organisations have the legal right to operate and manage services in low income areas.

- well-designed regulatory arrangements that promote improved transparency and accountability in decision-making.

For further guidance on incentives for serving the poor in PPP contracts, refer to WSP & PPIAF's publication: *New designs for water and sanitation transactions - making private sector participation work for the poor*, 2002. This document provides clear guidance for the various forms of PPP contracts.

Extracts from the performance contract between the Government of Uganda and the National Water and Sewerage Corporation (2000) are set out in Box 3.2. Note that there is a clear policy for serving the poor (100 per cent coverage) and an incentive in the form of potential subsidies from the GoU for 'social mission' work. But the overriding policy of financial viability and creditworthiness for NWSC is clear and is justified; otherwise the utility will not be able to raise sufficient funds for sustainable service provision.

More examples of policy level initiatives for improving incentive mechanisms for service providers are set out in chapter 4.

3.4   Potential utility initiatives and incentives for serving the poor

The service provider (utility), whether it is private or public or a combination of both, can provide incentives for low-income consumer groups and individual households. Examples of incentive mechanisms for these groups include:

Box 3.2. Performance contract for the NWSC water utility in Uganda

Selected provisions from the performance contract between the Government of Uganda and the National Water and Sewerage Corporation (2000) are as follows:

- **Supply/customer service objective:** The original objective of the GoU national water policy was to extend the use of safe water supplies to 100 per cent. It is generally expected to achieve this aim in 10 to 15 years from the present situation of 50 per cent coverage.
- **Financial objective:** It is accepted by both parties to this contract that the achievement of a financially viable and credit worthy NWSC is the overriding objective.

If investments are a 'social mission' imposed by GoU on NWSC, then the internal rate of re-turn of the investment must be determined in order to calculate the necessary GoU subsidy, to prevent the investment being a burden to NWSC.

---

a) low connection fees for pipe connections in poorer communities. The processing of new connections could be done with the help of community leaders and CBOs to ensure that the subsidy reaches the people for whom it is intended;

b) lower tariff levels for less convenient service options such as standposts, kiosks, shared connections, etc.;

c) providing materials for water connection in low-income settlements at subsidized prices and/or provide for payment in instalments;

d) opening utility liaison points in low-income settlements to provide services such as payment points, bill dispatch and technical/billing enquires;

e) investing in research in innovative options, such as local water storage arrangements, suitable for serving low-income settlements;

f) the inclusion of health promotion programmes to residents of low-income settlements. Refer to Box 3.3 for details about a programme in Ouagadougou's peri-urban areas;

**Box 3.3. Training youth committees to promote
water hygiene, Ouagadougou[1]**

The Office National de l'Eau et de l'Assainissement (ONEA) of Burkina Faso has empowered youth health committees in peri-urban areas of Ouagadougou and supported them in hygiene education and in promoting the use of clean water and sanitation facilities in the peri-urban ar-eas of Ouagadougou. The vision of the health committees is to become financially sustainable through funds raised through their activities. Youth health committees are trained prior to carry-ing out the following activities:

- Advising and raising awareness amongst the public in matters of health, hygiene, and the environment.
- Taking part in preventive health activities.
- Ensuring the cleanliness of the peri-urban areas.

These youth committees have become change agents in their communities, which has led to improved awareness of low-income communities. As a result, ONEA finds it easier to provide water services to these low-income settlements.

---

1. Source: Cooperation Francaise (1999)

g) encouraging local community-based labour during the process of connecting services in low-income settlements. This offer will not only reduce the costs of connections, but will also create employment for some members of the community; and

h) offering more flexible payment options that suit the needs of low-income consumers, such as group connections and community-managed water kiosks with regulated prices.

Examples of incentives offered to people using ground tanks in poorer communities in Durban are included in Box 3.4.

Box 3.4. Incentives offered by Durban Metro Water to ground tank users

Durban Metro Water & Waste of South Africa offers the following incentives to members of low-income communities who apply for a ground tank:

- The connection fee for the ground tank is about six times smaller than that of the conventional full pressure system.

- Unlike users of conventional water supply systems, ground tank owners are not charged a water deposit for security.

- The cost of materials is paid for in six monthly installations.

- Local private plumbers are trained at the Durban Metro water Services Training School, and were engaged in making water service connections in the low-income settlements.

- A community liaison officer is employed to handle issues connected with service delivery to low-income settlements.

3.5 Initiatives and incentives for working with CBOs, NGOs and SWEs

The service provider can, with the necessary support from government, provide incentives for community groups, NGOs, and small water enterprises. Examples of incentive mechanisms for these groups include:

a) Shared management arrangements with community groups that have potential benefits for both the utility and the community groups.

b) Effective partnerships with NGOs, such as letting contracts to NGOs or consultants for facilitation work and community capacity building.

c) Setting up of a department or section in the utility whose officers exclusively handle is-sues of water and sanitation services in poorer communities and working with community groups.

d) Supporting small water enterprises, including providing them with accessible points from which to collect their water. Provide relevant training to encourage good water handling practices. Perhaps offer start-up funds in terms of loans, to enable them to provide a better service to low-income communities. These issues are discussed further in the next section.

The service provider, whether private or public, could also provide incentives for its staff members to serve low-income communities. Examples of incentive mechanisms for staff include: raising status and pay of staff working in low-income areas and operation and maintenance activities; paying bonuses against carefully chosen indicators; and encouraging appropriate capacity building and less hierarchical ways of working.

3.6 Supporting small water enterprises

The range of different types of small water enterprises and some of the reasons that alternative water service providers command large market shares in many cities is discussed in Section 2.5.

Improvement of services levels to existing customers, and extension of services to potential customers in the urban areas, requires large sums of money in terms of capital expenditure. Currently, many utilities in low-income countries do not have the capacity to carry out huge expansion projects. Similarly, alternative water service suppliers in these cities do not have the capacity, on their own, to close the whole gap to meet the growing demands for improved services. It is therefore recommended that in order to accelerate service coverage to low-income settlements, governments should encourage utilities to collaborate with small water enterprises in order to deliver a better services.

Some of the constraints facing small water enterprises are:

- inadequate financing available for small water enterprises;

- lack of trust by the consumers concerning the source of the water that they buy from vendors, and therefore doubts about the quality of the product;

- high capital costs experienced by kiosk operators situated in areas where utility water main pipes are distant;

- lack of co-operation with utility officials concerning water collection points, meter reading frequencies, bill delivery periods, leakage repair periods, and other service-related problems; and

- lack of skills in bookkeeping practices.

It would be beneficial for the utility or municipality to assist in the formation of an association of SWEs in their city, or at least collaborate better with SWE groups, because it would enable them to:

- share experiences about service provision in poorly served areas and how they may be improved;

- to provide a forum to consider how the utility could support SWEs in providing improved services, particularly where the utility is unable to serve for some time; and

- to provide a forum for the utility/municipality to explore how SWEs could support utility initiatives for serving areas that do not have water mains.

There are a number of reasons why a positive market-orientated water utility would seek to collaborate with SWEs to improve services in areas where the utility cannot provide adequate services for some time. If consumers in such areas see that the utility is providing measures such as convenient water collection points for SWEs or vendors, and is publicizing the price it charges to the vendors with a view to keeping prices down, then those consumers will be more favourably disposed to the utility when it eventually starts to provide services in their community. In addition, community members would be pleased if utilities regulate vendor activities and provide training to SWEs to improve water handling and water quality for their customers.

Central or local government in conjunction with utilities can support such initiatives by undertaking activities such as:

- providing a legal framework that enables SWEs to provide water and sanitation services to serve in areas where there is demand for their services;

- facilitating SWEs to form associations with the support of utilities;

- facilitate partnerships between SWEs, water utilities and other major stakeholders; and

- build utility capacity to regulate operations of SWEs, to ensure services provided conform to minimum standards, although regulation of SWE prices is best done by increasing competition.

Ultimately, it is the responsibility of utilities to make the partnerships effective and thus improve their reputation amongst different consumer groups.

3.7   Performance measurement

Performance measurement against key indicators is an objective means of assessing actual utility performance and services to consumers, in comparison with the agreed corporate and government objectives. Effective performance measurement is essential for city-wide service improvements on a sustainable basis, as part of a strategic marketing approach and the benefits it offers include:

- more focused and better integrated performance data;

- easier identification of good and poor performance and its causes;

- strengthening of mechanisms for identifying the causes of good or poor performance;

- more focused institutional roles for assessing and acting on sector performance and a framework against which capacity building strategies and targets can potentially be developed;

- integration of all the 'tools' of performance measurement, e.g. operational monitoring, value for money review, technical audits, financial tracking studies, evaluation, etc.;

- improved information for assessing the effectiveness of water and sanitation policy and for enabling better policy making; and

- provides a more credible system for arguing for more resources for the water and sanitation sector and allocating resources within the sector.

Source: Thomson (2003)

Such potential benefits are very relevant both for utilities and for government departments who are concerned with broader national economic and social objectives, such as improving services to the poor. Government departments in their enabling role should therefore promote and expect effective performance measurement of utility services. The key performance measurement steps can be broken down into five components, as shown in the Figure 3.1.

What to measure?	How to measure it?	How to collect data?	How to analyse and present data?	What to do with the data?
•Review current objectives •Identify gaps •Remove unnecessary objectives and add new ones	•Match current indicators to objectives •Agree key performance 'theme', e.g. VFM, equity, effectiveness •Identify gaps and reduce overlap of indicators •Agree a focused and balanced set of 'core' indicators •Agree definitions •Set targets	•Determine which indicators are already measured •Identify gaps in data collection •Consider scope for rationalizing data collection exercises •Reassess indicators if data collection is too costly •Agree frequency of data collection •Allocate roles for data collection	•Determine what has to be analysed •Develop data analysis systems •Develop graphical and other clear ways of presenting data •Allocate roles for data analysis and presentation	•Allocate roles for acting on the data •Inform any need for additional evaluation and audit exercises •Feed results into the budgeting and planning cycle •Assess policy implications •Adjust future objectives if necessary

Figure 3.1. General steps in performance measurement[1]

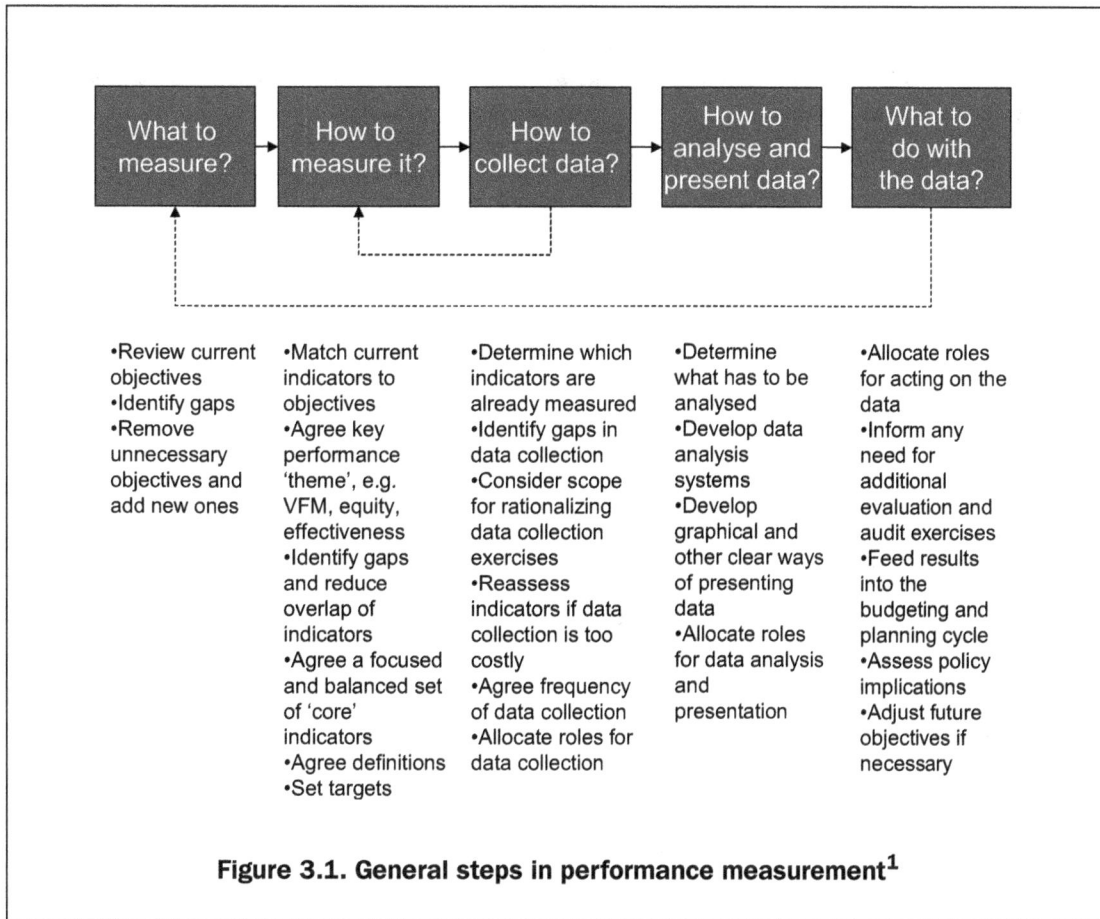

1. Source: Thomson (2003)

The key stakeholders such as government, utilities, regulator and consumer representatives have clear interests in ensuring that the performance measurement process is effective. This includes the activities listed in Figure 3.1 and the transparent exchange of information amongst the stakeholders.

Potential indicators for serving all consumer groups

The United Nations Department of Economic and Social Affairs (UNDESA) estimates that by the year 2015, 88 per cent of all the increase in global population will live in urban areas of low-income countries (UNDESA Population Division, 2001). Owing to the fact that the economic growth of these countries will often not match the population increase, a larger fraction of people in urban areas of low-income countries will live in low-income settlements. There is a need, therefore, to ensure that services are delivered to these low-income communities, in order to avert human suffering.

One of the ways national and state governments can ensure that services are provided to low-income settlements by urban water utilities is by entering into performance contracts or agreements with the service providers. In addition to the more general performance indicators for water utilities (referred to in Section 2.8), the governments can agree indicators that specifically cater for improvement in service delivery to the different consumer groups, including low-income settlements. These indicators can then be used to set targets and monitor trends in service levels amongst the different consumer groups or market segments. An sample format is shown in Table 3.1, which has separate columns for each market segment (based on work in Uganda and Mombasa).

Table 3.1. Service levels indicators and ratios by market segment

Example service delivery indicators	Example market segments			
	Residential houses and bungalows	Flats	One to three-room swahili houses	Informal settlements
1. Percentage of households with their own in house pipe connection				
2. Percentage of households with their own yard pipe connection				
3. Percentage of households who buy water from a neighbour				
4. Percentage of households using water kiosks or standposts				
5. Percentage of households who obtain water from alternative sources such as springs, wells and roof catchments				
6. Percentage of households who use more than one source				
7. Average total water consumption per person in the house - litre/person/day				
8. Average number of hours of utility water supply per day				
9. Average number of days per week that utility water is supplied				
10. Average time taken to collect all the water for the household each day from all sources (minutes)				
11. Average distance to nearest usable piped water source				
12. Average monthly household water bill				
13. Average vendor prices				
14. Percentage of both women and men satisfied with utility services				
15. Percentage of households who regularly use a functioning sanitation system within 20 metres of their residence				

Information against the indicators for the various market segments listed in Table 3.1 can be collected and updated on a regular basis, as a means of agreeing priority areas for action and setting targets for improvements in services. Note that information against all the indicators in the table should be obtained from well-designed consumer surveys. Annex 2 shows such a two-page consumer survey questionnaire that was field-tested in five towns in Uganda.

Rationale for proposed indicators

The rationale for the use of each indicator included in Table 3.1 is briefly discussed below.

Indicators 1 to 7 relate to service levels and are important for: assessing utility progress on service improvements; checking on value for money from investments; and for setting realistic targets. The emphasis is on actual use as reported by the consumers. Such indicators can also be used to prioritize new investments.

Indicators 8 and 9 show the average number of hours and days of water supply and are important for verifying progress on utility performance in service provision.

Indicator 10 shows the average time taken to collect all the household water each day from all sources, including travel and queuing time, and is an important investment outcome indicator. This is because if time savings are achieved, then there are clear opportunities for spending time on more productive activities that can be beneficial to a country's economy. Where there are high water collection times it suggests that there is a high demand for piped water.

Indicator 11 illustrates the average distance to the nearest usable piped water source and is useful for prioritizing new investments on extending the pipe distribution network closer to consumers. It can also be used to assess utility progress on service improvements, to check on value for money from investments, and to set realistic targets.

Indicators 12 and 13 concerning household expenditure on water and vendor prices provide support data for assessing people's ability and willingness to pay for improved services.

Indicator 14 on levels of satisfaction with utility service is important for assessing the utility's operational performance. It is suggested that separate data is collected for both men and women, because women often have very different experiences from men in aspects such as the collection and carrying of water.

Indicator 15 on functioning sanitation may be of limited interest to a water and sewerage utility, but it can be useful for policymakers concerned with sanitation in low-income areas.

If such information is regularly collected using well-designed consumer surveys that are representative of each market segment or consumer group, it is very beneficial. It enables both the utility and the regulator/government department to undertake ongoing effective monitoring against targets and analysing trends. Each utility and regulator would need to review the list of indicators that are most appropriate for each city.

Such a list of indicators can also be used on an area or zonal basis, where appropriate. Using a manageable number of market segments as a means of presenting the data, however, retains a poverty focus and is clear to the reader. When utilities use these indicators and agree to work towards reasonable targets, the process can act as an incentive to serve all consumer groups. Benchmarking between cities and towns against such indicators can also be used as an incentive for utility managers to take action.

3.8   Facilitating partnerships to serve the urban poor

One of the barriers urban water utilities find in serving low-income settlements is a lack of human and other resources for delivering services. Most staff in water utilities have received specialized training in engineering, accounts, and, to a lesser extent, in personnel management. Very few utilities have staff that are skilled in human development, sociology, social work, or community management. However, the work involved in serving the urban poor requires skills in human development issues, and therefore requires staff with the right skills to create and sustain dialogue with low-income community members. There is a need, therefore, for urban utilities to work in partnership with other organizations with capacity to work with low-income communities.

There are many stakeholders involved in community development activities, including the community health workers, non-governmental organizations, community-based organizations, local government, small water enterprises, etc, that are listed in Section 2.5. There is a need to create collaboration and synergy between the different actors, for the benefit of people living in low-income settlements. A dedicated government unit can be introduced to bring together the different actors to clarify and harmonize their roles. Such a unit can facilitate improved service provision to the urban poor by activities by:

*   building the capacity of the various stakeholders, including utilities who need a broader range of skills to work in informal settlements;

*   creating databases of roles, interests and capacities of 'actors' involved with the sector;

*   facilitating, monitoring and evaluating development programmes; and

*   setting guidelines for various financial issues such as tariff structures, capital funds, and remuneration/incentive schemes for the community members.

Partnerships with civil society organizations can also play important roles in helping regulation to become more pro-poor (Tremolet and Browning, 2002). For example they can:

*   help focus the attention of regulatory institutions on poverty issues;

*   assist in gathering information on the needs of the poor and make it available for regulators (and utilities);

*   create a more flexible, innovative and co-operative environment for developing rules better suited to the needs (and preferences) of the poor;

*   help partners understand each other's interests and constraints; and

*   develop a self-regulatory mechanism amongst the partners through regular meetings and exchange of information.

Further useful publications on partnerships such as 'Contracting NGOs' are contained on the Building Partnerships for Development (BPD) web-site: www.bpd-waterandsanitation.org. By encouraging such partnerships and developing capacities, the various stakeholders will have more incentives to develop joint initiatives for improving service in low-income areas. The potential facilitator roles of government are discussed further in Section 4.1.

3.9   Streamlining land tenure systems and access in low-income areas

Often, urban water utilities are faced with the difficulty of extending water and sanitation services to some parts of the cities or towns, particularly the low-income areas, due to complex land tenure systems. Land tenure systems affect provision of water services in several ways, such as the:

- ease of acquisition of land for construction of large water supply installations such as water treatment works, water storage tanks, sewage treatment works, and booster stations;

- acquisition of land for laying transmission and distribution mains; and

- ease of establishing clear and specific addresses for the end-user customers.

Different forms of land tenure systems exist in different countries. Similarly, a wide range of legislation to enforce the land tenure system is in place in various countries, with records of enforcement that are also variable. For the purpose of providing water services in an urban area, land tenure systems may be categorized as follows (Lyonnaise des Eaux, 1998):

- Public land, which is more easily accessed by squatters, and may be sub-divided into:

1.   Inalienable public land, which authorities cannot give up under any circumstances

2.   Alienable public land, which the authorities are willing to sell, rent, or grant as a concession. This type of land is attractive to potential squatters.

3.   'Available' public land, such as forests, national parks, etc, which is not allocated to anyone but is governed under the public land system. This is the type of land most easily accessible to spontaneous urbanization.

- Private land, which is more difficult for the squatters to access, and may be subdivided into the following categories:

1.   Properly and legally registered private land, which clearly has an owner, poses no specific problems as the utility can get into a transaction with the registered owner.

2.   Illegally registered private land, which may have been illegally allocated by local authorities with no reference to the central government land registry office. The best option is to follow up formalization of the registration procedures.

3.   Unregistered private land, which loosely comes under the sovereignty of a community or some other customary group, and governed under a law that is not necessarily laid down in writing. The boundaries of such land are not always clearly established.

It is easier for water utilities to acquire public land when they want to extend water and sanitation services. It is more difficult for the utilities to acquire land from private owners. In some instances, the costs of land compensation are so prohibitive that projects are abandoned altogether.

It is recognized that land tenure laws and systems are difficult to amend overnight. It is therefore suggested that governments should reassess and amend their legal frameworks to circumvent such land tenure constraints. Examples of initiatives to improve water services in illegal or unauthorized settlements include:

- regularizing appropriate unauthorised settlements;

- de-linking the rights to services from tenure status;

- seeking to resettle some people without legal title (WSP and PPIAF,2002); and

- compulsory acquisition of land by utilities to extend water services to low-income settlements, at a fee agreed by independent arbitration, according to the regulations;

- granting of 'easement' areas for the utility to construct and maintain water and sewerage facilities, with appropriate levels of compensation for disruption paid to land owners, according to the regulations. The utility requires ongoing free access to the facilities constructed for maintenance and rehabilitation purposes, with planning restrictions enforced that prohibit building over pipelines; and

- acquiring land to extend water services to low-income settlements by the central or local government, i.e. the government pays the landowners and owns the land over the public water facilities.

Flexibility should be encouraged to explore which potential solution is the most appropriate in each case. The legal framework should support the preferred options for action. Such initiatives make it easier for utilities to work in unauthorized settlements and hence are likely to increase their willingness to work in those areas.

3.10   Health and hygiene promotion for low-income communities

Although the necessary infrastructure may be constructed in low-income settlements using a combination of loans and grants from central governments and international donor organizations, cost recovery remains a pre-requisite for sustained service delivery. However, for some members of the low-income community, water and sanitation services are not necessarily a high priority for the well being of the family. Many family heads do not consider payment for potable water supply a priority in the family budget. Reasons for this include:

- lack of awareness about the relationship between water and sanitation, and hygiene practices to health;

- lack of knowledge on the effects of poor quality and low quantity of water and poor sanitation practices on the health of the family; and

- lack of understanding and appreciation of the changing natural environment, owing to high population densities. Some families who in the past relied on traditional water sources with limited health hazards have not recognized the increasing level of pollution of these sources.

There is therefore a need for central and local governments to facilitate and support various agencies involved in providing hygiene promotion activities to low-income communities. This can create increased demand for improved water services and thus make the marketing of different options in poor areas more viable. Hygiene promotion may be enhanced in a number of ways:

- Learn to understand existing hygiene practices in low income-communities, identifying the risk practices, the group that carries out the practices, and the channels used for communication. This is best done using participatory approaches that enable community members to analyse community practices and identify possible solutions.

- Develop hygiene messages and promotion strategies based on what community members (men, women, children) perceive as the advantages of the alternative safe practices. Evidence has shown that conventional hygiene promotion efforts focusing on better health are unlikely to have an impact on the uptake of improved hygiene behaviour.

- Involve school-aged children and youths through the introduction of health and promotion in the national school curriculum. Activities can also be facilitated and support by the formation of school health clubs. Competition in various hygiene promotion activities such as community drama could be encouraged amongst schools. Experience has shown that children can be effective agents for change and can bridge the gap between the school and the community.

- Involve existing community groups and decision-makers such as youth clubs, church groups, women groups, elders, teachers and preachers in hygiene promotion activities.

- Use existing channels with a wide coverage such as radios, megaphones, and churches for mass campaigns, especially during the anticipation of major outbreaks. Local radio stations can be facilitated and supported to carry out these campaigns at relevant intervals. An example case where this proved effective is summarized in Box 3.5.

- Develop strategies and indicators that will enable communities to monitor or measure the progress and impact of hygiene promotion activities. Policymakers could encourage this by organizing quarterly competitions and awarding prizes to winning communities.

For guidance on setting up a hygiene promotion programme refer to:

- *Happy, Healthy and Hygienic: How to set up a hygiene promotion programme* by Valerie Curtis and Bernadette Kanki, 1998

- *Hygiene Evaluation Procedures: Approaches and methods for assessing water-and sanitation-related hygiene practices* by Astier Almedom, Ursula Blumenthal and Lenore Manderson. 1997

By promoting the use of enough water of adequate quality and explaining the advantages to community members, there are better prospects of poorer families increasing their demand for and willingness to pay for good utility water services.

3.11 Empowering low-income communities

Empowerment is the extent to which people in the community can and will make decisions on their own in their own environment. Empowerment affects the way of working, the way of organizing, and the relationship between community members and the external public. It involves providing communities with enough relevant information, and giving them more autonomy to take decisions on matters that affect their communities. Empowerment entails a change in the design of authority and responsibility limits among the communities.

Box 3.5. Community radio promotion work in Kampala[1]

Sebina Zone in the Kawempe Division of Kampala City Council is a low-lying area, mainly inhabited by low-income earning residents. The houses are unplanned, and prone to seasonal flooding, depending on the intensity of the seasonal rains. Although there is a secondary water main pipe passing along the main road to Gayaza, there are no tertiary mains teeing off the secondary main. Most residents of Sebina rely on traditional water sources such as wells and protected and unprotected springs, as the price of water sold by water vendors is beyond the reach of most people.

During the El-Niño period (1997-8), the skies opened up for days on end, and Sebina zone flooded for a relatively long period, submerging all the traditional water sources. Because of the poor sanitary situation in the community, the quality of water completely deteriorated, resulting in outbreaks of diarrhoeal diseases in the area. The Local Council committee and the local community leaders held an emergency meeting and mapped out a strategy of averting the situation through immediate hygiene education.

The Local Council Committee immediately bought a public address system with a large powerful loudspeaker, which they hung on a high pole mounted in the centre of the zone. The committee immediately earmarked a health worker, one of their residents, to carry out hygiene education on 'Radio Sebina'. Within a couple of weeks, the positive impacts of the health campaigns were realized when incidences of diarrhoeal diseases were tremendously reduced.

The community leaders realized the benefit of the local community radio in information dissemination, so long after the El-Niño floods, the community radio has not only stayed, but has grown in sophistication to carry out other functions, such as radio announcements and entertainment. This innovation has spread to a few other low-income settlements in Kampala City such as Bwaise.

1. Source: Kayaga (2002)

Giving the communities more decision-making powers will enhance the participatory capacity of community members and hence improve prospects for community groups to enter into useful shared management options with the local water utility. To achieve this, a participatory process is required; this consists of letting different actors work together towards a common goal. Participation by community members leads to a greater sense of responsibility and better management of water services in low-income settlements (Brikke and Rojas, 2000). If the communities have the capacity, the role of the service provider will be reduced to facilitating the process of designing, learning and decision-making.

The government has an important role to play in empowering people living in low-income settlements. The central or local government should create an environment that is conducive for the following values to take root (Brikke and Rojas, 2000):

-   Democracy, every man and woman have the opportunity to participate without prejudice

-   Responsibility, each actor is responsible for his /her experiences and behaviour

-   Cooperation, members of the communities work together to achieve the same collective goal

One way of enhancing empowerment of the communities is through capacity-building processes. Governments may build the capacity of the communities by:

- consulting with the communities and creating a legal framework that clearly spells out the roles and responsibilities of the community members, and how they relate to other stakeholders in the provision of services;

- training selected members of the communities in leadership skills, advocacy, basic bookkeeping and financial management; and

- ensuring that water utilities are accountable to the community members, in respect of their service deliverables and activities in the low-income settlements.

3.12 Poverty reduction programmes for low-income communities

- In order to provide a sustainable service to low-income communities, there is a need to in-stitute adequate cost-recovery measures on the users. Many consumers in low-income set-tlements will have low ability to pay. The government may intervene to reduce poverty as part of broader development programmes that are not just confined to the water sector. Such initiatives can improve consumers ability to pay for services. A few examples are outlined below (Brikke and Rojas, 2000):

Box 3.6. Micro-credit: The Grameen Bank in Bangladesh[1]

The Grameen Bank in Bangladesh was created with the assumption that the absence of access to financial resources is one of the major causes of poverty. Its mechanisms rely on a system of reciprocity and mutual guarantee that replaces the system of material guarantee. Groups of five candidates with similar economic status are formed. In order to obtain credit, candidates have to follow a two-week course during which they are exposed to the philosophy, regulations and the procedures of the Grameen Bank.

Candidates have to submit simple plans showing how reimbursements for loan repayment will be made. To start with only two candidates get a loan. If the reimbursement procedures are correctly followed, then the other candidates can borrow as well. However, the goods acquired through the loan remain the property of the bank until the loan has been totally reimbursed. Reimbursements are usually done on a weekly basis, for a period not exceeding a year. 56 per cent of credits are given to women, and the rate of reimbursement is above 95 per cent.

---

1. Source: Brikke and Rojas, 2000

- The local government may facilitate local leaders or community groups to collect voluntary contributions through public meetings, bazaars, lotteries, and similar social activities. The success of this option depends on the whether the community has a tradition of fundraising.

- The local government may facilitate communities to own collectively income-generating projects such as co-operative shops, the profit from which may be used to pay for water service improvements.

- Households may be encouraged to contribute to cost recovery in kind, by providing la-bour for trench digging, transport, pipe laying, or provision of local materials.

- The local government may support micro-banking schemes among the low-income communities. Loans obtained may be used to extend services to the individual households. Box 3.6 shows an example of a successful micro-credit scheme in Bangladesh.

- Central government and local authorities may allocate part of their budgets for construction of water supply facilities to low-income settlements. This, however, depends on the government policies and availability of funds.

- The government may acquire grants from international donors to finance capital works to extend water services to low-income communities, perhaps as part of broader development programmes.

Chapter 4

Government roles in service provision to all consumer groups

4.1   Policy overview

Increasingly governments are realizing that there is a need to develop policies and action plans that address the needs and demands of poor and disadvantaged groups who experience inadequate services. This is evident from national poverty reduction strategy papers and similar outputs in many developing countries. A key question is how to implement such polices? The marketing approach advocated in this document provides a viable means for achieving improved urban water services for the poor and other consumer groups, provided the enabling environment is both supportive and appropriate. This chapter addresses the question of how governments can help to develop such an enabling environment, building on the ideas of increasing incentives in the previous chapter.

Most governments now focus their efforts on 'enabling roles' rather than undertaking service provision themselves. Figure 4.1 depicts the separation of the enabling agencies (government and regulators) from the service provider roles, as well as the relationship with users, as part of the New Public Management approach.

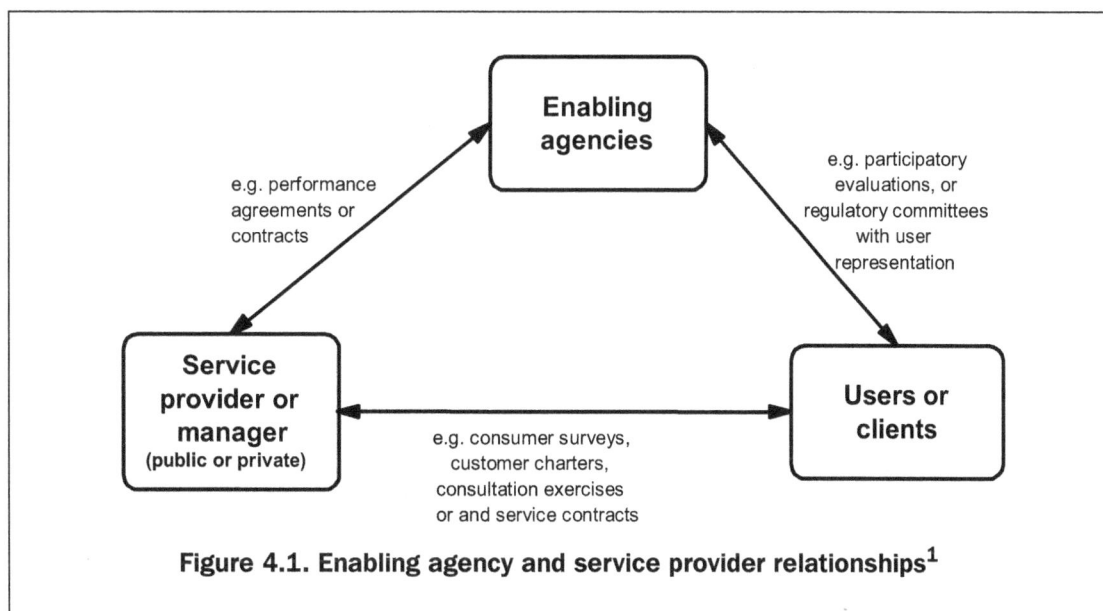

Figure 4.1. Enabling agency and service provider relationships[1]

1.   Source: adapted from Hobley and Shields (2001)

The enabling agencies can develop performance agreements or contracts with the service provider, but must give them sufficient autonomy to allow them to manage effectively. This encourages the use of more performance-based management. The service provider can develop 'beneficial exchange relationships' with the users or customers, for example a clear message can be: 'We (the service provider) will provide better services if you (the customer) pay higher water charges'.

Experience from around the world shows that the service provider role - such as managing urban water services - is best left to dedicated, autonomous, commercially and consumer-orientated water utilities who collaborate with other stakeholders such as small water enterprises.

The key government enabling roles can usefully be broken down into four main groups: governance, regulation, facilitator and financier, as is depicted in Figure 4.2.

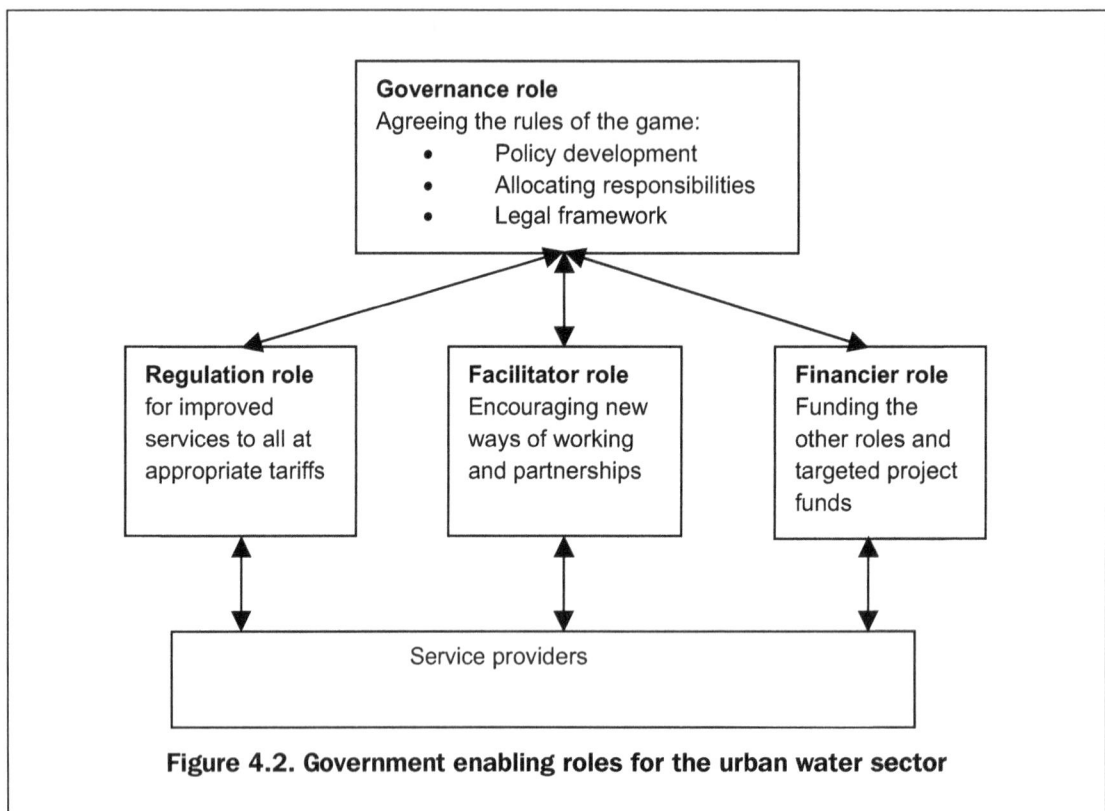

Governance role
Agreeing the rules of the game:
- Policy development
- Allocating responsibilities
- Legal framework

Regulation role
for improved services to all at appropriate tariffs

Facilitator role
Encouraging new ways of working and partnerships

Financier role
Funding the other roles and targeted project funds

Service providers

Figure 4.2. Government enabling roles for the urban water sector

These enabling roles and the associated issues for supporting services to low-income groups are discussed in the following sections.

Governance - agreeing the rules of the game
Policy development
Governments need to regularly review their policies to assess whether they are the best means of improving performance in the sector. Other policy options need to be considered, building on lessons learnt in-country and elsewhere. Relevant policy areas include:

- enabling poverty reduction and improved services to all consumer groups;

- achieving full cost recovery and financial viability of service providers;

- promoting demand-responsive approaches to service provision;

- sector-wide approaches (SWAp) where donor funding and support contributes to the development of the entire sector and not just individual projects;

- supporting private sector participation (both formal and informal providers);

- supporting community participation in decision-making and flexible management options; and

- decentralization that supports other policy initiatives.

Policy reviews and the policy options that are developed should incorporate the views of key stakeholders and informants. Agreed policies then inform other governance tasks such as allocating responsibilities and legal frameworks, as well as other enabling roles such as the regulation, facilitator and financier roles.

Allocating responsibilities

In many low and middle-income countries, water utilities operate in an environment where the roles and responsibilities of various stakeholders in the water sector are not streamlined or clear. In some instances, the same arm of government acts as a policymaker, facilitator, regulator and service provider at the same time. This situation does not promote efficiency, effectiveness and accountability in the water sector. It is therefore the responsibility of central governments to carry out policy reforms with the aim of creating a conducive legal and policy framework that enables water utilities to provide efficient, sustainable, affordable services to the population, underscored by sound governance, efficient investment management, and cost-effective delivery systems.

Early in the process there is a need to rationalize the roles of various agencies in terms of policy setting, facilitation of capital funds, asset ownership, regulation, setting of standards, and service delivery. Overlapping or fragmented roles and responsibilities can lead to a lack of action and should therefore be avoided.

Allowing water supply organizations or utilities as much organizational and financial autonomy as possible enables them to manage effectively in a consumer-orientated manner, with minimal bureaucratic constraints, so that they can develop and implement strategic marketing or business plans. Providing such autonomy may of course necessitate reallocating responsibilities between different organizations and departments.

With regard to sanitation, there are many benefits in making the water utility responsible for sewerage services, including the advantage of a combined water and sewerage bill, that provides more incentives for payment of sewerage charges. Because of its individual, discrete characteristics, however, on-plot sanitation does not require the skills of a network utility. Traditionally sanitation has also been co-ordinated by Municipal Departments rather than water utilities.

A key consideration is who should undertake the regulatory function (described below). These functions are often done by various government departments, and there is some lack of clarity of roles. Establishing independent regulator(s) for aspects such as improving service levels linked to water and sewerage charges and environmental issues can encourage better accountability, transparency and a more professional approach. Regulators are particularly appropriate when complex PPP contracts are being developed, such as Lease and Concession contracts. A separate regulator also has potential and similar advantages for overseeing public utilities. Regulators also need to be equipped with the capacity to ad-dress services to the poor (WSP and PPIAF, 2002).

The regulator(s) need appropriate objectives, authority and a clear remit or boundaries to their responsibilities. For example, should the regulator implement a Universal Service Obligation (USO) for all consumers? If so it must be clear how this will be funded (ibid). The regulator or government department can encourage the utility to agree yearly targets for service improvements and tariffs for all consumer groups or market segments, including low-income areas. This is a constructive means of gradually achieving a USO. Flexible definitions of coverage and service levels need to be encouraged, so that more choice in service options can be encouraged.

The use of Consumer Services Committees and other similar forums can be an effective means of allowing the views of different consumer groups to be represented when key decisions are being made by utilities and regulator/government departments.

Water sector reform also benefits from strengthening partnerships with various other stakeholders in the water sector, such as civil society institutions, (e.g. NGOs, CBOs and unions) and potentially with vendor or small-scale provider associations, all of whom have a stake in the sector, with the objective of creating improved collaboration and synergies.

The overall allocation of roles and responsibilities for the sector needs to compliment government policies such as moving towards full cost recovery for water services and poverty reduction. The emerging policies and distribution of roles then need to be captured in revised legislation.

Improving accountability and transparency

As policies are developed and responsibilities allocated, an important guiding principle is to improve both accountability and transparency amongst the key stakeholders. Both factors are critical to gain and maintain the trust of users and investors. They are founded on: (i) clear roles and responsibilities; (ii) independent audit and monitoring; and (iii) open disclosure of information.

Accountability is defined as a set of relationships among service delivery actors with five key features (World Development Report, 2004):

- **Delegating:** Explicit or implicit understanding that a service will be supplied

- **Financing:** Providing the resources to enable the service to be provided

- **Performing:** Supplying the actual service

- **Having information about performance:** Obtaining relevant information and evaluating performance against expectations

- **Enforcing:** Being able to impose sanctions for inappropriate performance or provide rewards when performance is good.

Paying careful attention to these five aspects can enable improvements in accountability and hence improve performance. The relevant government departments are normally responsible for delegating responsibilities to the respective stakeholder institutions, although further delegation to other organizations usually occurs. All stakeholders are concerned with having appropriate information, although a regulator can take a leading role in ensuring that there is a *transparent* exchange of relevant information. Regulators (where they exist) are also expected to undertake the enforcing role in an unbiased manner.

One important means of improving transparency and accountability is through effective performance measurement (which is discussed in Section 3.6), followed by the dissemination of results and key information to concerned stakeholders. Four relationships of accountability have been identified (World Development Report, 2004):

- politicians to citizens or users;

- the service provider to the state;

- the frontline professions to their employer (management); and

- the service provider to the citizens or users.

Transparency and accountability need to be continually addressed for all the four relationships listed above if genuine improvements to services for all consumers are to be achieved.

Legal frameworks
Appropriate legislation needs to be developed or amended to improve services to low-income consumers, covering aspects such as:

a) Allowing private sector involvement and competition
Enabling the private sector to participate in water service provision can introduce much-needed incentives and skills. However, private sector operators should not be given exclusive rights to provide water services, which would prevent alternative providers from offering services in poorly served areas.

b) Water laws and water resources management
Providing a framework in necessary to ensure that adequate water supply is available for current and future needs of all consumers. The use of groundwater and other water sources should not, however, be unduly restrictive, so as to allow people to use alternative sources where it is feasible and where there is a demand.

c) Land tenure issues
The legal framework should support improved services to poor communities who may lack legal title to their land, where governments have a poverty reduction strategy. Flexibility should be encouraged to explore potential solutions such as: regularizing unauthorized settlements, delinking the rights to services from tenure status, or seeking to resettle some people without legal title (WSP and PPIAF, 2002).

d) Services to the poor and subsidies
Improving services to the poor is best achieved by exploring every relevant aspect of the government's and utility's work to determine viable means of making it easier to improve services to each consumer group. Funds available for subsidies are generally diminishing so it is important to prioritize those limited funds. A general principle is to *subsidize*

access not consumption. For example it is better for utilities to subsidize cheaper service options such as water kiosks, standposts or shared connections, that give a reduced level of service compared to in-house private connections.

e) Environmental and health standards

Government legislation in these areas can act as an effective driver for improvements. For example, there could be requirements to clean up polluted watercourses, and activity that often impacts more on informal settlements, which tend to be located in low-lying areas. The requirement of a minimum water supply availability standard such as 20 litres per per-son per day (WHO water quality standards), can also be used as a basis for service providers to develop new programmes. Such minimum standards should inform selection of priority areas, but new projects are likely to be more sustainable if they are also responding to demand based on consultation with water users.

Regulation

Good regulation is a means of impartially improving accountability and transparency to enable more effective service provision. The regulatory process has to separate policy-maker and provider and preserve its own independence (World Development Report, 2004). Key issues related to regulation and serving poor consumers incorporating marketing approaches that are worthwhile pursuing include:

a) Ensuring responsiveness to consumer needs

Regular well-designed consumer surveys that obtain good quality data from all consumer groups or market segments (see Section 2.5) enable utilities to work towards improved customer satisfaction and hence improved cost recovery. Where expansion and improvement of services are being contemplated, willingness-to-pay surveys and other demand-assessment techniques such as 'PREPP' contribute to the development of better investment programmes that are more likely to be funded when viable financial projections are produced based on the demand assessment. Such survey information is also invaluable for a regulator in agreeing performance and tariff levels.

b) Flexible technical and service standards

To allow incremental improvements to water services to a greater number of consumers, flexibility in service standards should be encouraged to allow the development of appropriate service, shared management, and payment options that meet the needs and preferences of different consumer groups, as discussed in Chapters 1 and 2. This is likely to require re-viewing national and regional technical standards and policies to ensure that they do not unduly inhibit the introduction of such viable options.

c) Performance planning and monitoring

To encourage effective planning and monitoring of utility activities for all consumer groups, the use of appropriate indicators for assessing progress and setting reasonable targets is recommended. Typical indicators are set out in Sections 2.8 and 3.6, including the use of market segments as a means of assessing performance in all groups including the poor.

The use of strategic marketing plans can enable utilities to plan and monitor all their work in a more comprehensive and demand-responsive manner on a sustainable basis. Where such documents are well developed they can provide an invaluable basis for well-informed regulation.

d) Safety net regulations for the poor

Poor consumers often pay high prices for water from vendors, or they incur high coping costs in terms of the time they spend collecting water, or dealing with the adverse effects of poor quality water. So rather than insisting on very low tariffs for poor consumers - which will limit the incentives for utilities to serve low-income communities - it is better for a regulator or government to encourage utilities to collect data on services, experiences and perceptions in poorer areas, with a view to expanding services on a sustainable basis, with some cross-subsidization between different service options.

e) Development of essential infrastructure

Supplying new or poorly served areas with adequate piped water supplies invariably requires investment in new treatment, transmission and distribution infrastructure. A regulator and the concerned government department needs to satisfy themselves that the utility (private or public) is developing and implementing adequate and viable plans to service such areas. A strategic marketing approach is a way of developing plans that are sufficiently comprehensive.

f) Promote asset serviceability and efficiency over time

To achieve adequate and sustainable services in the long term, utilities should be encouraged to have good asset management arrangements that ensure that the condition and performance of the infrastructure assets is maintained. This is particularly important when the end of a PPP contract is approaching, so that adequate maintenance, rehabilitation and re-placement occurs throughout the contract.

g) Support for Asset Management Plans

Encouraging and supporting water utilities to develop and adhere to Asset Management Plans (AMP) enables good information on the location, condition and performance of utility assets in all areas of a city or town to be stored and retrieved. This is an important component of providing adequate and sustainable services to all consumer groups.

h) Agreeing projected water and sewerage tariff policies

This is a key area for regulation and needs to be linked to service improvements. Allowing utilities to charge cost-recovering tariffs is not only necessary for sustainable services, it provides the basis for investing to meet future demands and population growth. These issues are discussed further in Section 4.5.

Whether a separate regulator is established, or this work is done by designated sections in government departments, it is beneficial if their functions are carried out both comprehensively and impartially. Strengthening of the regulatory regime is important and can be done through activities such as:

• sub-dividing functions such as water and sanitation performance and tariff regulation, as well as environmental and water quality regulation;

• strengthening technical capacity for the different functions of regulation;

• ensuring the independence of the regulator through an open and publicly account-able process of recruitment and publication of studies and decisions;

• backing up the regulatory process with the necessary legal framework;

• funding of the regulatory activities through a dedicated budget; and

- considering forming a multi-utility regulatory framework, where applicable.

Such measures can improve the accountability and transparency of the regulatory functions and thus contribute to effective development of the sector.

Facilitator and financier roles

A government can usefully act as a 'facilitator' to encourage key sector stakeholders to improve social inclusion (Bosch et al., 2001) and to pursue innovative options for collaboration and management with key partners. Some typical 'facilitator' activities include:

- Arranging national/regional surveys of the roles and capacities of different 'actors' in the sector, including utilities, government departments, small-scale providers, CBOs, NGOs, consultants, donors, and contractors with a view to improved collaboration.

- Supporting the development of a comprehensive performance measurement programme, including consumer surveys, to inform future policies and investment decisions.

- Co-ordinating the development of policies and strategies for improving water and sanitation services to low-income urban areas, amongst key stakeholders at all levels, that lead to effective action plans that are implemented. This is discussed further in Section 4.3.

- Agreeing potential roles for the different stakeholders and the implications of new or revised roles.

- Assessing capacity development requirements for different sector 'actors' so that the agreed policies and strategies can be implemented.

- Co-ordinating sector development projects or programmes, that may be pilot projects or state/nationwide initiatives. Such programmes may have some donor funding from a Sector Wide Approach (SWAp) or from discreet programmes.

- Seeking the collaboration of other ministries and government departments in supporting the development of the water sector and services to poor consumers.

- Monitoring and evaluating the implementation of strategies to improve services in low-income urban areas, providing timely feedback to partners.

- Supporting service expansion and negotiations for grants and soft loans.

- Supporting sector research activities, particularly to determine lessons from new approaches.

Government and donor funds for development projects are limited and need to be carefully targeted, as utilities will hopefully move towards full cost recovery for service provision. Governments therefore need to be selective in their 'financier' role to maximize value for money and to enable other stakeholders to fulfil their roles. Potential areas for funding that support a pro-poor enabling environment include:

- sector studies and policy development;

- funding of the 'facilitator' role activities listed above;

- targeting limited capital funds on services for low-income areas, provided there is clear demand for those service/management options that are on offer;

- capacity development for different partners and stakeholders, particularly where they take on new or revised roles;

- supporting regulation activities where they are not funded by PPP contracts; and

- supporting sector research activities.

Funding of capacity development is important during a reform process. Where capacity building is required for different stakeholders such as utilities, NGOs, consultants and private contractor/operators, it is preferable if those stakeholders at least provide some funding for their training so that they demonstrate their commitment to participate in the reform process.

4.2   Supporting private sector participation

If private sector participation is to be developed on a substantial basis that benefits all consumer groups, it will be necessary to develop an enabling environment at city, state and national level, addressing key constraints. Some countries see private sector participation as a key part of their strategy to improve services. For example, refer to Box 4.1 for a summary of Uganda's urban water sector policies.

Box 4.1. Uganda's urban water sector polices

The policy of the Government of Uganda is to limit the role of government in water sector to that of policymaker, facilitator and regulator, thus leaving service delivery to the private sector as much as possible. Consequently, a water sector reform study was commissioned in 1999, and mandated to advise on the reform process, using the following sector objective as a guide:

- Service coverage - to achieve universal coverage for safe water and appropriate sanitation by the year 2010

- Sustainability - to achieve sustainability of service delivery. This includes reduction of government subsidies if they remain necessary, or improving the efficiency of such subsidies. The successful introduction of public-private partnerships is a cornerstone to this goal

- Affordability - to ensure that a basic adequate level of service is affordable via low-cost delivery and implementation of a subsidy and tariff framework that is equitable and beneficial to the poor

- Water as a social and economic good - water should be managed in the best way, bringing consequent benefits such as improved health to the citizens, as well as infrastructure and economic development.

In addition to the general reform and policy initiatives described in this chapter, specific measures to develop private sector participation (PSP) that benefits all consumer groups include:

- **Studies to identify the most suitable PSP strategy** and type of contract, that is based on good quality information on *'where the utility and services are now'*, given the prevailing internal and macro-environment, and where the utility(s) want to be in the future.

- **Making the contracts work for the poor** needs to be considered at all stages of contract development, including providing appropriate incentives and funding for the private operator to extend services to low-income areas. Further guidance is provided in *PSP and the Poor* (Sohail et al., 2003) and *New designs for water and sanitation transactions - making PSP work for the poor* (WSP and PPIAF, 2002).

For those organizations contemplating private sector participation, they can refer to the World Bank 'Toolkits for Private Sector Participation in Water and Sanitation' (1997), which provides comprehensive guidance on the range of PSP contracts. For those utilities or municipalities contemplating smaller Service and Management contracts, *Contracting Out Water and Sanitation Services - Guidance Notes for Service and Management Contracts in Developing Countries* (Sansom et al., 2003) provides practical information on contract development and monitoring.

4.3   Translating policies and strategies into actions

In order to accelerate water supply and sanitation service provision to low-income settlements in urban areas, there should be both technological and institutional innovations and new approaches at various levels. A key step in this process is the formulation of national policies and strategies that need to incorporate the concerns of the various stakeholder groups. Box 4.2 shows extracts from a national policy on service provision to low-income settlements developed by the Government of Zambia.

In order to build on what is already being done and to capture broad support, it is important to involve all key stakeholders in the provision of services to low-income settlements such as water authorities, government departments, municipal councils, active non-governmental organizations, community-based organizations, small-scale independent providers, donors, consultants, contractors/operators and training providers. Figure 4.3 is a flow chart of a typical participatory process that can be followed in the development of national policies and strategies and that leads to effective action plans. Note that there are feedback loops in the process, in recognition of the fact that it is an evolving iterative process, where improvements can be made over time, based on lessons learnt.

It may also be necessary to review policies in the light of implementation experiences. Key activities in the national action plan for peri-urban areas developed in Zambia in 2001 are set out in Box 4.3.

It is worth noting that Zambia has an independent water regulator, the National Water Supply and Sanitation Council (Nawasco), to support utility and municipal improvements in services to the poor. Action plans such as that summarized in Box 4.3, are useful in creating an enabling environment at the national level, but further policies and plans are also required at the city level, and this is discussed in the next section.

Box 4.2. National policy for peri-urban water and sanitation in Zambia [1]

The Ministry of Local Government and Housing in Zambia, with the support of the Water & Sanitation Pro-gram (WSP), has developed a national strategy on peri-urban water and sanitation. Key elements in the strategy are highlighted below.

Overall development goal of the strategy: **'adequate, accessible, sustainable and safe water supply and improved sanitation services are available and effectively used in all peri-urban areas in Zambia'**.

The target for the minimum level of water service is 30 litres per person per day up to a walking distance of 200m. To achieve these goals will require careful planning and management of services. The 'strategy objective' to achieve these goals is therefore: **'to establish a framework for effective and efficient planning, implementation and management of water supply and sanitation in peri-urban areas'**.

Policy measures in the strategy include:
- Services shall be provided on the basis of a *demand/responsive approach* in partnership with community organizations and the community itself.

- *Sanitation and hygiene promotion* shall be integrated into water supply projects in order to give greater emphasis to sanitation.

- *Water utilities are to have overall responsibility* over WSS systems in peri-urban settlements within the local authority areas under their jurisdiction.

- *Selection of communities to be assisted* shall be on the basis of expressed demand for better services and a willingness by the communities to make contributions (cash or in kind) to investments and to bear full running costs.

- *Community participation and management* shall be encouraged in partnership with NGOs and community groups.

- *The interests of women, children and the vulnerable* shall be considered and protected in the design and management of services.

The strategy also included priority actions which were later developed into a 'Peri-Urban WS&S Action Plan'. The key actions are summarized in Box 4.3.

---

1. *Source:* Ministry of Local Government & Housing, Zambia (2001)

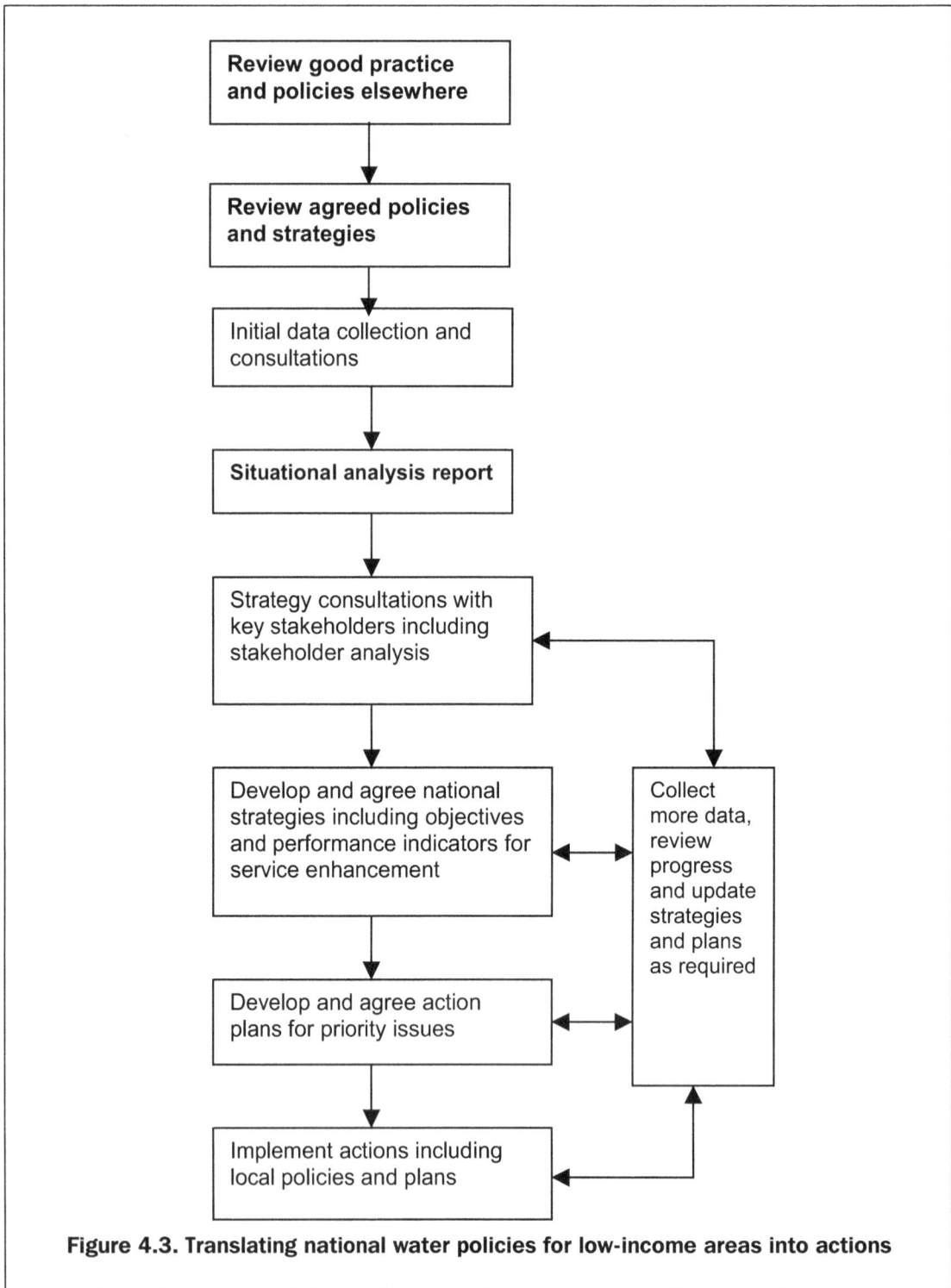

```
┌─────────────────────────┐
│ Review good practice     │
│ and policies elsewhere   │
└─────────────────────────┘
            │
            ▼
┌─────────────────────────┐
│ Review agreed policies   │
│ and strategies           │
└─────────────────────────┘
            │
            ▼
┌─────────────────────────┐
│ Initial data collection  │
│ and consultations        │
└─────────────────────────┘
            │
            ▼
┌─────────────────────────┐
│ Situational analysis     │
│ report                   │
└─────────────────────────┘
            │
            ▼
┌─────────────────────────┐
│ Strategy consultations   │
│ with key stakeholders    │◄────────────────┐
│ including stakeholder    │                  │
│ analysis                 │                  │
└─────────────────────────┘                  │
            │                                 │
            ▼                                 │
┌─────────────────────────┐    ┌─────────────────┐
│ Develop and agree        │    │ Collect         │
│ national strategies      │◄──►│ more data,      │
│ including objectives     │    │ review          │
│ and performance          │    │ progress        │
│ indicators for service   │    │ and update      │
│ enhancement              │    │ strategies      │
└─────────────────────────┘    │ and plans       │
            │                   │ as required     │
            ▼                   │                 │
┌─────────────────────────┐    │                 │
│ Develop and agree action │◄──►│                 │
│ plans for priority issues│    │                 │
└─────────────────────────┘    └─────────────────┘
            │                            │
            ▼                            │
┌─────────────────────────┐             │
│ Implement actions        │◄────────────┘
│ including local policies │
│ and plans                │
└─────────────────────────┘
```

Figure 4.3. Translating national water policies for low-income areas into actions

Box 4.3. National action plan for peri-urban water and sanitation in Zambia[1]

The Ministry of Local Government and Housing in Zambia, with the support of the Water & Sanitation Pro-gram (WSP), has developed a 'Peri-Urban WS&S Action Plan' that was derived from the national strategy on the same subject (see Box 4.2). Key action points are summarized below:

Key issues for action:

Policy and legal framework
- Revision of the *national water policy* to include the unique characteristics of peri-urban areas.
- Develop guidelines for supporting community participation and management.
- Develop national programme for *regularization and legalisation of informal settlements* including *publicizing the regularization process* in order to involve communities in all stages of planning and execution of the programme.
- *Ownership of community WS&S facilities* to be clarified. Community ownership to be at least in pro-portion to the level of their contributions.

Institutional issues
- Establish a properly resourced *unit in the Ministry to facilitate and co-ordinate* WS&S programmes in peri-urban areas.
- Establish *stakeholders' forum* to co-ordinate overall peri-urban development including NGOs and donors.
- The *legal and institutional framework for the various community-based institutions* shall be reviewed and revised.
- Formulate guidelines to *clarify roles of utilities, local authorities and community organizations* for service provision.
- *Community-level institutional support* including capacity building, effective administration, information flows and monitoring and evaluation systems for use by communities. Draw lessons from existing community-managed schemes.
- Establish and maintain *databases of WS&S and socio-economic information* for specific peri-urban areas.
- Establish and maintain a database of *technology options* to improve choice.

Financial issues
- Develop guidelines for *remuneration and incentives scheme* for community members.
- Formulate/collate guidelines for willingness/ability-to-pay surveys and tariff setting.
- Establish a 'capital revolving sanitation fund' for funding higher levels of WS&S services.
- Establish 'revolving sanitation fund' with initial grant funding.
- Harmonize the flow of funds to peri-urban WS&S projects.

Note action points concerning policy measures listed in the previous box on the national strategy are not repeated here. Responsibilities were allocated for each action point to specific organizations, with a time-frame for the completion of the activity.

1. *Source:* Ministry of Local Government and Housing, Zambia (2001)

4.4   Agreeing the utility's objectives

Corporate objectives are at the heart of the strategic marketing process, since they describe the direction, priorities and the relative position of the organization in its market. The objectives help to create guidelines for marketing plans, since the output of the corporate planning process acts as an input into the marketing planning process (Brassington and Pettitt, 2000). Specific objectives are normally presented in terms of different kinds of targets. A common objective of progressive water utilities is to improve service provision to customers while meeting the utility's financial objectives. Many utilities in developing countries will be operating in an environment where large proportions of the potential customer base, especially the low-income customers, are currently not served. There will be a need for the utility's top management to review and agree the utility's objectives, particularly with regard to serving the apparently 'less profitable' poor.

Organizations often summarize their objectives in the form of mission statements. Examples of two mission statements from African water utilities are provided in Box 4.4.

Box 4.4. African utility mission statements

The mission statement for the National Water Conservation and Pipeline Corporation (NWCPC) in Kenya (NWCPC, 1999):

The corporation is committed to providing high quality water to its customers at an affordable price and at a reasonable profit to the corporation.

Mission statement for National Water and Sewerage Corporation (NWSC) in Uganda (Kayaga and Sansom, 2001):

To be financially a self-sufficient organization developing and providing water supply and sewerage to customers at an affordable price.

It is interesting to note from those mission statements from utilities in Kenya and Uganda that they only refer to their customers. But what about the people who are not their customers - the people who do not have their own pipe connection? Potential utility objective statements are set out in Box 4.5. Mission statements will also need to take account of cur-rent government policies and the current state of services in the utility's service area.

Box 4.5. Potential utility objectives

Key strategic marketing objectives for progressive water utilities:
• Provide adequate and reliable water and sewerage services whilst improving customer satisfaction through continuous service enhancements to all consumer groups.·

• Through the development of cost-reflective tariffs and targeted subsidies achieve a reasonable return on the capital employed as an efficient provider.

A summary of key provisions of the Lusaka Water and Sewerage Company's policy in 2001 that emerged after the national policies and action plans for serving peri-urban areas is provided in Box 4.6. Other cities, with different working environments, may develop quite different local policies.

Box 4.6. Lusaka's policy on water and sanitation in peri-urban areas[1]

Lusaka Water and Sewerage Company (LWSC) have developed a document that sets out its policy on water and sanitation in peri-urban areas, settlements or 'compounds' that are categorized as low-income and high-density. They were encouraged to do so following the agreement of the national strategy on the same subject. The rationale of the LWSC document is:

'Due to the multiplicity of public and private agencies, as well as the presence of numerous donors and NGOs, co-ordination of water and sanitation services is required to derive the greatest benefits from limited budgets in an area where the challenges are very great. The LWSC is one of the major actors in this field, and it has therefore taken the initiative in preparing this document.'

The key areas covered by the document are:
(a) Statutory legal responsibilities of LWSC - including the provision of water and sewerage services in the area of jurisdiction of Lusaka city council and to exercise control over water sources.
(b) The institutional framework - including:
- the specified wards where peri-urban informal settlements are located;

- agreed ToR for resident development committees (water committees);

- listing of the peri-urban areas and their legal status;

- listing of the water and sanitation service providers in Lusaka

- a summary of the roles that LWSC will undertake, including: O&M of water distribution up to the meters, collaboration with community groups, bulk supply of water to edge of some peri-urban areas, training of plumbers for community management of water distribution, etc.; and

- the roles of other institutions such as the city council who deal with sanitation aspects other than sewerage.

(c) Options for service provision Details and sketches are provided.

---

1. *Source:* LWSC (2002)

4.5   Water tariff and subsidy review

Water utilities in many low-income countries are often unable to collect enough revenue to cover both operation and maintenance costs and the capital funds required to improve the system. The level of water tariffs are often too low to meet all the utility's full costs. Another common problem is that tariff structures penalize some consumer groups unfairly.

Approval of the water tariff is generally the responsibility of the central or state governments in many low-income countries. Therefore the onus is on governments to regulate water utilities to improve revenue collection through viable water tariffs, hopefully through an independent regulatory regime. Increasingly, efficient urban water utilities in low-income countries are applying tariffs designed to cover return on investments and major capital expenses. The following text provides guidance on tariff setting and the provision of subsidies.

General principles

The determination of tariff policies should seek to address both commercial and social welfare concerns. It is beneficial if revised tariff levels can be finalized based on mutually agreeable principles. The simple but comprehensive 'AESCE' principles (which we pronounce 'ace') are outlined in Box 4.7.

Box 4.7. Developing tariff policies using the 'AESCE' principles

When considering appropriate tariff policies, AESCE is a useful memory aid:

Adequate. The average tariff should be cost reflective, which means it should cover the cost of 'OPEX' - operating costs, 'CAPEX' - capital maintenance (infrastructure renewals and depreciation) and the cost of capital - to ensure that loans can be repaid and future investment financed whilst the existing system is maintained.

Equitable. The required level of revenue should be allocated between customer groups in a fair and equitable for manner both for the poorer members of the community and the different levels of service options, relative to the costs they impose on the system and to reflect social welfare objectives to achieve public health.

Simple. The tariff structure should be simple for the utility to administer and easy for customers to understand. Customers usually display greater willingness to sustain payment of water bills when they understand the bills.

Conserving. The tariff structure should influence consumption in such a way that customers are able to purchase enough water to meet their needs without being wasteful.

Enforceable. The utility should be able to enforce the tariff through viable sanctions such as court action, disconnections, etc. Tariffs that cannot be enforced are unlikely to be sustainable.

To ensure adequate tariff levels are achieved, calculations need to include proposed future loans and investments. *Book 2* provides some guidance on calculating tariffs using the Average Incremental Costs (AIC) approach based on future investment proposals.

In many countries rising block tariffs have been introduced to try to ensure that consumers of small amounts pay less per kilolitre than larger consumers, as well as to encourage the conservation of water. In practice problems have emerged with this system, as is described in Box 4.8.

So rising block tariffs do not always achieve the 'equitable' component of the 'AESCE' principles, as described in Box 4.8. Some more specific ideas for tariff setting and subsidies are:

a) Get the tariff level and the tariff structure right to help all consumers, including the poor.

b) Subsidize access *(or lack of access)*, not consumption.

c) Subsidy delivery mechanisms should be targeted, transparent and triggered by household indications of demand.

d) New information is often required to evaluate whether a proposed tariff or subsidy will hurt or help poor households.

e) Because tariffs and subsidies require modifications over time, decisions that must be made about social equity concerns should be incorporated in the tariff and subsidy revision process.

Source: Water and Sanitation Program and PPIAF (2002) and Whittington (1992)

A brief case study from Manila in Box 4.9, highlights how tariff increases can help the poor by providing more funds for extending services to unserved areas.

Box 4.8. Block tariffs to subsidize the poor?[1]

Many urban water utilities use a block system of tariffs for metered households. The principle is that families using less water pay less per kilolitre up to a threshold consumption per month. More affluent households who use more than the threshold, pay more per kilolitre of water consumed above that threshold, in accordance with the next tariff 'slab'. This is in recognition of the fact that water is a social as well as an economic good. Problems can arise in developing countries where a number of poor families use the same metered connection, illegally or otherwise, and they use more than the threshold amount, thus paying more for their water. Under such circumstances poor families can pay more with a block tariff system than if there was a flat tariff per kilolitre consumed. Such disparities can encourage a climate of not paying. In Santiago, Chile they have dealt with this problem by not subsidizing the poor through lower water charges, e.g. with block tariffs, but providing instead separate well-targeted subsidies. Other cities who suffer water shortage problems wish to retain the block tariff system to send economic signals to consumers to conserve water. In which case they will need to carefully design and market service options and tariff levels to ensure equity for multi-family pipe connections.

---

1. *Source:* DFID (1998)

Box 4.9. Hiking tariffs to help the poor in Manila[1]

Winnie Flores, one of about 5 million people without access to piped water in Manila, pays 900 pesos a month for 6 m3 of water from small water enterprises, while many connected to piped water pay about 160 pesos a month for 30m3. It would be much cheaper for her to have a piped connection. With the introduction of private sector participation in 1996, the winning bids of the two successful companies who won the concession contracts were 57 per cent and 26 per cent of the pre-bid Manila water utility tariff. The contract conditions encouraged keeping the tariffs low, but did not have provisions for increasing access to piped water to the poor. For a couple of years the government resisted the tariff increases that would enable extension of the piped network to serve poor areas. The government finally capitulated and allowed the necessary tariff adjustments in order to extend services to unserved areas. The clear lessons are that tariff increases can help the poor, and that it is important to get the policies right for all consumer groups.

---

1. *Source*: Summary of a case study in Asian Water Supplies - Reaching the Urban Poor by A.C. McIntosh (2003)

When negotiating tariff levels there are a number of key issues to be borne in mind, which are summarized in Table 4.1.

Table 4.1. Key issues for setting tariffs

Issue	Potential impact on tariff policy
National policy priorities	National or state policy might impact on tariff setting. For example, if government policy is to move to full cost recovery, including capital costs, this should impact on tariff increases.
Cross subsidization of poorer communities	If an aim is to improve equity, tariffs can be set at different levels for different user groups and service options.
Consideration of the cost of water supply and sewerage	As populations and demands increase, utilities invariably have to consider using more distant water sources. The full costs of using such sources, as well as the bulk water supply and distribution networks, need to be included in the tariff calculation.Sewerage and appropriate wastewater treatment is invariably higher in cost than water supply. Where sewerage programmes are envisaged, the full costs should be considered in determining tariff levels.
Willingness to pay of communities	This is an important factor and is becoming increasingly accepted as a key element of tariff setting. Tariffs can be raised for those individuals / communities who are willing to pay more for water supply.
Willingness to charge	Policymakers/politicians may often be unwilling to increase water charges because they perceive that tariff increases are likely to be unpopular with the public. Orientation of policymakers is often required to demonstrate the benefits to all stakeholders of generating adequate funds through increased tariff levels.

New medium term tariff levels need to be considered when doing financial projections for future investments. Where substantial tariff increases are required, they should preferably be within the willingness-to-pay levels derived from surveys. Increases are best done on an incremental basis that are acceptable to key stakeholders. Addressing the 'willingness to charge issue' mentioned in the above table is critical, so careful thought is required in developing a strategy for advocating tariff increases.

Agreeing tariffs for different service levels

By offering different options to different customer groups there are opportunities to set lower water prices for options that are less convenient to consumers, or where options cost the utility less to provide, or where subsidies to the poor are proposed. For example, a water kiosk that is managed by a community group has less operational costs for a utility than a kiosk managed by the utility itself. Trickle feed supplies are cheaper than full water pressure, so tariffs can be lowered accordingly to capture people's willingness to pay. A simplified calculation for balancing projected income for each service option with utility costs is set out below:

Let us assume that the average calculated tariff for financial sustainability for a city is, say, US$1.00 per cubic metre and that the average consumption per household is 10 cubic metres a month. For 50,000 paying households in a city, the total domestic water income for the utility will be:

$1.00 X 10 cubic metres X 12 months X 50,000 households = **$6 million**

(Average tariff X Water volume sold = Total domestic water sales income)
(excluding connection charges, etc.)

If the total expected income from commercial/industrial and other institutions in the city is $2 million at the same tariff level, then the total projected yearly income for financial sustainability is:

$6 million + $2 million = **$8 million**

The tariff levels for each service option offered will need to be adapted to generate this same level of income ($8 million) as is shown in the simplified calculation in Table 4.2 below. Note the tariffs can be adjusted to match the WTP of customers for each option offered, as well as reflecting the reduced costs of provision for the different service levels offered to poor or unserved communities.

Table 4.2. Balancing service option tariffs with income

Service option	Proposed option tariff ($ per cubic metre)		Projected sales volume (cubic metres of water)		Projected income from each option
Utility-managed water kiosks	$0.80	X	300,000	=	$0.24 million
Community-managed water kiosks	$0.60	X	400,000	=	$0.24 million
Yard connection with storage tank and trickle feed	$0.80	X	500,000	=	$0.4 million
Individual house connection with 12 hours supply to roof tank at full pressure	$1.00	X	4.8 million	=	$4.8 million
Commercial/ industrial users	$1.16		2 million	=	$2.32 million
			Total income		$8.0 million

Such an approach allows for some limited cross subsidization between different service options; that is, subsidizing the lack of access and not consumption. The figures in Table 4.2 do not include sewerage charges which would need to be added for household supplies where on-plot disposal is not feasible. The calculation is rather simplified, as demand for water will vary with price, but it offers a basic approach to differentiating service options at appropriate prices, in order to maximize both income and the number of satisfied customers.

Other important issues that need to be considered in the setting of water charges are:

- Where possible, good quality water meters should be provided, read and used to determine water bills, as this encourages water conservation and it is a fair means of determining water charges.

- Water bills should include any sewerage charges, preferably reflecting the full sewerage costs.

- Whether to charge full connection charges up front, or to spread the recovery over a period of time, so that connection fees may not be prohibitive to the prospective customer, particularly in low-income communities.

- To charge a monthly service fee to cover some of the services such as reading of meters, instead of charging a minimum charge, which if too high can encourage wastage of water.

- To charge a disconnection/reconnection fee that is not prohibitive, because high fees can encourage illegal water usage.

- Regular yearly tariff increases are recommended to move towards full cost recovery and to allow for inflation, using appropriate formulae.

4.6   Government support for revenue collection

High outstanding water bills that have accumulated over a long period of time is a common problem. In some cases, the revenue collected may not even be sufficient to cover operation and maintenance activities. In most cases, the revenue collected does not provide for capital funding. The government can support the utility's revenue collection drive in a number of ways. Examples are given below:

- Government departments and institutions consume a significant proportion of water supplied by urban water utilities in low-income countries. It is common for government departments and institutions to be the largest debtors to the water utilities. If the government pays for water services promptly it sets a good example and improves water utility revenues. The process of payment may be simplified further by creating a central coordination unit to receive, verify and process water bills for all government departments and institutions.

- Wastage of water supplied to government departments and institution is common, due to poorly maintained installations. When the water supply installation is maintained well, water that would otherwise have gone to waste is channelled to other needy people.

- Government should strengthen public health byelaws and create a conducive legal environment to enforce the byelaws that prohibit operation of businesses and residence in urban centres without suitable water supply and sanitation provisions.

- Government should support efforts by water authorities to disconnect water supplies of commercial/industrial premises and residential properties for perpetual non-payment of water rates.

4.7   Government support for service expansion

The central government may support water utilities to improve their infrastructure and increase service coverage in a number of ways. In addition to the marketing approaches advocated, a few examples are mentioned below:

- **Responsibility for historical loans:** Many urban water utilities previously took on loans for infrastructure improvement. These loans carry grace periods during which investments were supposed to have been completed, prior to the completion of the pay-back period. However, due to various factors, the investments carried out may not have realized the benefits envisaged in the original investment plans. These factors may range from poor design, poor construction, lack of investment balance between production capacities and distribution networks, political interferences, and/or poor organizational policies and structures. As a result, some water utilities may not be capable of dealing with their loan portfolio. In order to keep to the overall objective of providing services to all consumers, it is recommended that governments participate in any negotiations for restructuring those loans.

- **Acquisition of grants and soft loans for expansion of services:** To maximize funding for poor or un-served areas, governments should seek to acquire more donor grants for water utilities to expand their service coverage. They can also assist in negotiating for soft loans on good terms from international banking institutions, and provide a guarantee. The strategic marketing approach can assist in making a case for such grants and loans. Furthermore, it would be beneficial for governments to waive the requirement of on-lending the grants and soft loans to water utilities at higher interest rates.

- **Use of international debt relief funds from the HIPC Initiative for expansion of services to the urban poor:** These funds are available for countries that fall under the category of Highly Indebted Poor Countries (HIPC), which are exclusively meant for poverty alleviation. These funds can be accessed and used for improving service coverage to urban low-income settlements. These funds could be used for tertiary pipeline ex-tensions, storage expansions, and for subsidizing house connections for the benefit of low-income families.

- **Performance contracts/agreements with utilities/municipalities:** Whether an independent regulator is in place or not, it is beneficial to have a performance con-tract/agreement between the regulator or government and the utility, to ensure financial viability of the utility and improving services to all consumer groups, in line with agreed targets. The contract/agreement would typically include key objectives, performance against key targets and the tariff policies. To achieve a poverty reduction focus, the performance contracts can be used to track improvements to services in low-income areas.

- **Well-designed PPP contracts** that have specific provisions to encourage the operator to extend services to new areas and customers. It will be necessary to have agreed investment plans for service extension that compliment the performance requirements in the contract.

4.8   Research and dissemination of lessons

The task of ensuring that there is universal service coverage in urban areas of low-income countries is substantial. If this task is to be fulfilled, there is a need to bring about changes at the sector utility and community level, and at the household level. The challenge is greater for water utilities as far as provision and extension of services to low-income settlements is concerned. There is a need to carry out research and develop low-cost and technologically appropriate service options that are acceptable to the consumers. Research activities demand significant investments, which the service providers may not always be able to afford. Government can therefore provide a framework and funds for such research activities. Examples where further research funding is required are:

- implementing poverty reduction strategies in the urban water and sanitation sector;

- lessons for institutional reforms that enable more of a focus on improved services to low-income areas, including regulation and government's facilitatory roles;

- benchmarking activities to evaluate and map out best practices in other low-income countries, including the process of documentation and dissemination of information to the various stakeholders; and

- research in the use of low-cost water supply and sanitation service options suitable for and acceptable by low-income communities.

Governments can usefully co-ordinate local research activities conducted by various stake-holders to ensure that all key areas of concern are being addressed. It will be beneficial to report on further lessons learnt from using marketing approaches in different water and sanitation sector contexts. Key findings should be disseminated both locally and internationally. By continuing to share the important lessons from the use of marketing approaches and serving all consumer groups, wider take up of these ideas and increased benefits can be expected.

Glossary

7ps	Product, Price, Promotion, Place, People, Process and Presence.
Buying decision process	The conscious and unconscious thinking process a consumer goes through before deciding to buy a good or service.
CBO	Community based organisations who may take an active part in decision making or management of water and sanitation services in their area.
Competition	In this document any water source or provider of supply that detracts a consumer from using a utility provided source or which deters the consumer from buying water from the utility.
Consumer demand	An expression of desire for a particular service, assessed by the investments people are prepared to make, over the lifetime of the service to receive and sustain it.
Contingent valuation	A demand assessment technique. Several options (each associated with a range of prices) are described to a sample of potential users who then indicate their preferences. It can be used to assess people's maximum willingness to pay for services that are not currently available. The technique requires specialist skills and is more cost effective in high-density urban and peri-urban areas.
Coping strategy	A behaviour or practice used to sustain or improve a livelihood.
Customer orientation	Turning attention to the needs of the customer and using the organisations resources to satisfy those needs.
Customer value chain	The process of knowing, targeting, selling and servicing customers.
Demand	An expression of desire for a particular service, assessed by the investments people are prepared to make, over the lifetime of the service to receive and sustain it.

Effective demand	Demand for a good or service expressed by a user's willingness to pay in terms of a monetary or economic contribution.
Existing practices	How people obtain, pay and use water now.
Experiences	Accumulated knowledge, feelings and occurrences. Familiarity and know-how.
Focus group	A small group of individuals with a similar social, cultural or economic background, brought together with a facilitator to explore a particular issue.
Informal settlements	In this document this is the generic term used to describe where the urban poor reside. It includes illegal slums, informal settlements, compounds, low-income areas, townships, peri-urban areas, unplanned zones and shanties.
Latent demand	Demand that is only revealed after it has been stimulated (that is open to techniques that unlock demand).
Level of service	Or service level) describes the quality of the service provided. It refers to the physical infrastructure or technology used: stand post, communal tap, a yard tap, a house connection.
Low-income area	In this document this is the generic term used to describe where the urban poor reside. It includes illegal slums, informal settlements, compounds, townships, peri-urban areas, unplanned zones and shanties.
Marketing	There are a number of definitions for marketing including: 'The management process responsible for identifying, anticipating and satisfying customer requirements profitably'.
Market segmentation	Splitting consumers in to groups defined by common characteristics, for example social status or housing type for the purposes of understanding the main consumer groups and targeting service options.
Marketing mix	The way a competitive position relative to other options is achieved.
NGOs	Non-governmental organisations typically work with community groups in low income areas, while liasing with government and service providers with a view to

improving services and reducing poverty. They usually have good facilitation skills and experience of working in informal settlements.

Non-revenue water

The difference between water produced and water sold to customers expressed as a percentage of water produced.

Non-utility water sources

Including protected and unprotected springs, rainwater collected in buckets/cooking pots, shallow wells.

On-selling

Water sold from an individual house connection to neighbours. The utility charges one person only.

Perceptions

The way in which people see a situation determining how they are likely to behave.

Poverty

Poor quality of life combining low income, poor health and education, deprivation in knowledge and communications, and the inability to exercise human and political rights.

Preferences

Judgment that something is 'best for purpose' from the user's perspective.

Price & service differentiation

Process of developing appropriate service options (technology and management) at appropriate prices based on the needs of different market segments - customer groups, on a sustainable basis.

Small water enterprises

SWEs are also called small scale independent providers and are part of the informal private sector who provide water services to consumers, particularly in areas where complete water services are not provided by a utility.

Social marketing

The application of marketing techniques to stimulate demand. The underlying motivation is to reduce exposure to environmental health risks rather than a profit motive.

Strategic marketing

Marketing as a management process whereby the resources of the organization are used to satisfy the needs of selected consumer groups in order to achieve the objectives of both parties. Strategic city-wide planning is usually required in the urban water context.

Tri-sector partnerships
In this document partnerships between government, the private sector and civil society.

Utility-direct sources
Including public stand post, kiosk, communal yard taps.

Utility-indirect sources
Including handcart vendors, bicycle vendors where water is taken from a utility supplied source.

Want
A desire for a good or service that goes beyond a felt need in that it may satisfy a person's longer term needs or aspirations, but may not be price sensitive, hence the need to consider consumer demand.

Willingness to charge
The low willingness of key stakeholders such as politicians to increase tariffs to adequate levels is common, hence the need to encourage an increased 'willingness to charge' using appropriate advocacy strategies.

Willingness to pay
The financial or economic contribution that people are willing to make to receive and sustain a particular service.

Willingness to pay surveys
A variety of survey techniques such as the contingent valuation method (CVM) can be used to illicit the maximum amount that respondents are willing to pay for a given service level.

References and Bibliography

Bosch C., Homman. K., Rubio G.M., Sadoff C. and Travers L. (2001) *Water, sanitation and poverty - Poverty reduction strategy sourcebook (draft)*, World-bank.org/poverty/strategies/chapters/water/wat0427.pdf

Brassington, F. and Pettitt, S. (2000) *Principles of Marketing*. Second Edition, Financial Times/Prentice Hall, UK.

Brocklehurst C., and Evans, B. (2001) *Serving Poor Consumers in South Asian Cities*. The Water and Sanitation Program-South Asia, India.

Coates S., Sansom K.R., Kayaga S. (2001) 'PREPP - improving utility watsan services to low income communities'. Paper presented at the 27th WEDC Conference, Lusaka, Zambia, August 2001.

Coates S., Sansom, K.R., Kayaga S., Chary S., Narender A., and Njiru, C. (2004) *Serving All Urban Consumers - A marketing approach to water services in low and middle-income countries. Book 3: PREPP - Participatory Ranking Experiences Perceptions and Partnerships*. WEDC, Loughborough University, UK.

Collingnon B. and M. Vezina (2000) 'Independent water and sanitation providers in African Cities'. Water and Sanitation Program, Washington, USA

DFID (1998) *Guidance manual on water and sanitation programmes*, WEDC, Loughborough University, UK

Farnham, David, and Horton, Sylvia (1996) *Managing the New Public Services*. 2nd Edition, Macmillan Press Ltd, UK

Franceys, R.W.A.F. and Sansom, K.R (1999) 'The Role of Government in Adjusting Economies: Paper No.35 - India Urban Water Supply'. DFID, University of Birmingham, UK.

Gould, J. and Nissen-Peterson, E. (1999) *Rainwater Catchment Systems for Domestic Supply*. Intermediate Technology Publications, London.

Heskett, James L. (1986) *Managing in the Service Economy*. Harvard Business School Press, Boston, Massachusetts.

Hobley M. and Shields, D. (2001) 'Governance and institutional structures', paper presented to the DFID Seminar on Governance and Sustainable Livelihoods, Birmingham.

Howard, A.G. (2002) *Water Quality Surveillance - A reference manual.* WEDC, Loughborough University, UK.

Inocencio, A. (2002) 'Manila Water and Sewerage Concessions', in Weitz, A., and Franceys, R., *Beyond Boundaries: Extending services to the urban poor.* Asian Development Bank, Manila, Philippines.

Jones, Peter (ed.) (1989) *Management in Service Industries.* Pitman Publishing, Longman Group UK Limited, London.

Kamalie, A. (2001) 'Marketing and service differentiation of the Water and Sewerage Authority, Lesotho'. MSc thesis at IHE, Delft, The Netherlands.

Katko, T.S. (1991) *Paying for Water in Developing Countries.* Tampere University of Technology, Tampere, Finland.

Kayaga, S. and Sansom, K. (2004) *Serving all urban consumers — Book 5 — Sample strategic marketing plan for water services in Kampala City, Uganda.* WEDC, Loughborough University, Loughborough, UK.

LWSC (Lusaka Water Supply and Sewerage Company) (2002) 'Policy document on water supplies and sanitation in peri-urban areas of Lusaka', unpublished document, Zambia.

Lyonnais des Eaux (now Ondeo) (1998) *Alternative Solutions for Water and Sanitation in Areas with Limited Financial Resources.* Paris.

McIntosh, A.C. (2003) *Asian Water Supplies: Reaching the urban poor.* Asian Development Bank and International Water Association, IWA, London.

Narender, A. Chary, V.S. and Sansom, K.R. (2004) *Serving all urban consumers — Book 6 — Sample strategic marketing plan for water services in Gun-tur, India.* WEDC, UK

Nickson, R.A. (2001), 'Establishing and Implementing a joint venture: Water and Sanitation Services in Cartagena, Columbia. Building Municipal Capacity for Private Sector Participation', Working Paper No. 442 05, GHK International, London

Njiru, C. and Sansom, K.R. (2004) *Serving all urban consumers — Book 4 — Sample strategic marketing plan for water services in Mom-basa and Coast Region of Kenya.* WEDC, UK.

Obel-Lawson, E., and Njoroge, B.K. (2000) *Small Service Providers make a Big Difference*: Field Note Number 5. UNDP-World Bank Water and Sanitation Program, Nairobi, Kenya.

Revels, C. (2002) 'Business planning for small town water supply', paper presented at the Addis Ababa Conference on Water Supply and Sanitation (WSS) Services for Small Towns and Multi-Village Schemes, Ethiopia, Water and Sanitation Program, World Bank.

Sage, R. (2002) *Meaningful Relations*. Water Services, UK.

Sansom, K.R., Franceys, R., Njiru, C. and Morales-Reyes, J. (eds) (2003) *Contracting Out Water and Sanitation Services: Book 2: Case Studies and Analysis of Service and Man-agement Contracts in Developing Countries*. WEDC, Loughborough University, Loughborough, UK.

Sansom, K.R., Franceys, R., Njiru, C. and Morales-Reyes, J. (2003), *Contracting Out Water and Sanitation Services - Book 1- Guidance Notes for Service and Management Contracts in Developing Countries*, WEDC, Loughborough University, Loughborough.

Sansom, K.R., Coates, S., Njiru, C. and Franceys, R. (1999) 'Strategic Marketing to Improve Both Water Utility Finances and Services to Poor Urban Water Consumers'. Discussion Paper, WEDC, Loughborough University, UK

Sansom, K.R., Franceys, R., Njiru, C., Kayaga, S., Coates, S. and Chary, S.J. (2004) *Serving All Urban Consumers: A marketing approach to water services in low and middle-income countries. Book 2 - Guidance notes for managers*. WEDC, Loughborough University, UK.

Sohail, M. et al (2004) Series of publication on: *PPP and the Poor*. WEDC, Loughborough University, UK. http://www.lboro.ac.uk/wedc/projects/ppp-poor/index.htm

Thomson, M. (2003) *Uganda water and sanitation sector: Performance measurement framework report*. WELL Resource Centre, WEDC, UK.

Tremolet S. and Browning, S. (2002) *The interface between regulatory frameworks and partnerships - Public, private and civil society partnerships providing water and sanitation partnerships to the poor*. Business Partners for Development - BPD (http://www.bpd-waterandsanitation.org).

Water and Sanitation Program (WSP) and PPIAF (2002) *New Designs for Water and Sanitation Transactions: Making Private Sector Participation Work for the Poor*. WSP, Washington DC, USA.

Water Utilities Partnership, Africa (2000) *Performance indicators of some African water supply and sanitation utilities*. WUP, Cote D'Ivoire.

Water Utility Partnership (WUP) Africa (2003) *Better water and sanitation for the urban poor - good practice from Sub-Saharan Africa*, WSP and WUP, Cote d'Ivoire.

Wedgwood, A. and Sansom, K.R. (2003) *Willingness-to-pay surveys: A streamlined approach - Guidance notes for small town water services*. WEDC, Loughborough University, Loughborough, UK.

Whittington, D. (1992) 'Possible adverse effects of increasing block water tariffs in developing countries', Economic development and cultural change, USA.

Whittington, D and Swarna(1994) 'The economic benefits of potable water supply projects to households in developing countries', Staff paper No.53, Department of Environmental Sciences and Engineering, University of North Carolina at Chapel Hill.

Wilson, R.M.S. and Gilligan, C. (1997) *Strategic Marketing Management.* 2nd Edition, Butterworth-Heinemann, UK.

World Bank (date) Field Note Number 5, UNDP-World Bank Water and Sanitation Program, East and Southern Africa Region

World Bank (1997) *Toolkits for Private Participation in Water and Sanitation.* World Bank, Washington, DC.

World Bank (2000) www.worldbank.org/html/extdr/pb/pbpoverty.htm

World Bank (2004) *World Development Report 2004: Making Services Work for Poor People.* World Bank, Washington, DC.

Zambia Ministry of Local Government and Housing, 'Peri-urban water supply and sanitation strategy', unpublished document.

Annexes

Annexe 1: Sample strategic marketing investment plan for Kampala (2001)

Year	0	5	10	15	20	25	TARIFF
HIGH INCOME AREAS							Merit Billing hse conn. above 6m3 p.m.
Service Level 1:Full pressure							Government/Institutional
Total Number of Accounts	13960	16460	20960	32260	56260	83260	Small Scale Ind/Comm up to 30 m3 p.m.
Consumption (m3 per year)	3566780	4475029	6063627	9930720	18428554	29020381	Commercial/Ind activities > 30 m3 p.m
Av. Consump. Per Account per Month	21.3	22.7	24.1	25.7	27.3	29.0	Public tap rate
Lifeline billing		355536	452736	696816	1215216	1798416	
Merit Billing		2406948	3265827	5355438	9950047	15686451	
Total Billing		2762484	3718563	6052254	11165263	17484867	
MIDDLE INCOME AREAS							
Service Level 1:Full pressure							
Total Number of Accounts	13960	21160	28660	48460	115460	187460	
Consumption	3566780	5752832	8291200	14917629	37820137	65339426	
Av. Consump. Per Account per Month	21.3	22.7	24.1	25.7	27.3	29.0	
Lifeline billing		457056	619056	1046736	2493936	4049136	
Merit Billing		3094230	4465582	8044778	20420057	35318066	
Total Billing		3551286	5084638	9091514	22913993	39367202	
Service Level 2:12-hr household supply							
Total Number of Accounts	0	6000	12000	20500	30500	40500	
Consumption	0	1387559	3139791	6068659	10215463	15347320	
Av. Consump. Per Account per Month	0.0	19.3	21.8	24.7	27.9	31.6	
Lifeline billing		129600	259200	442800	658800	874800	
Merit Billing		743357	1687285	3270112	5517854	8307376	
Total Billing		872957	1946485	3712912	6176654	9182176	
Service Level 3: 12-hr yard tap supply							
Total Number of Accounts	0	2500	5000	6000	7000	8000	
Consumption	0	361343.5	817654	1110121	1465332.8	1894731	
Av. Consump. Per Account per Month	0.0	12.0	13.6	15.4	17.4	19.7	
Lifeline billing		54000	108000	129600	151200	172800	
Merit Billing		190489	433210	590766	782833	1015702	
Total Billing		244489	541210	720366	934033	1188502	
Service Level 4:Shared connection							
Total Number of Accounts	0	2500	5000	6300	7000	7350	
Consumption	0	867224.4	1962370	2797504	3516798.6	4177881.6	
Av. Consump. Per Account per Month	0	28.9	32.7	37.0	41.9	47.4	
Billing		260167	588711	839251	1055040	1253364	
LOW INCOME AREAS							
Service Level 5:Ground tank							
Total Number of Accounts	0	4000	8800	10900	13400	18400	
Consumption	0	319184	783841	1091398	1502045	2292290	
Av. Consump. Per Account per Month	0	6.6	7.4	8.3	9.3	10.4	
Billing		95755.2	235152.3	327419.4	450613.5	687686.9	
Service Level 6:Community kiosk							
Number of Accounts	0	500	850	1060	1540	2540	
Consumption	0	239388.1	456246.4	638933.4	1030586.4	1877450.2	
Av. Consump. Per Account per Month	0	39.9	44.7	50.2	55.8	61.6	
Billing		47877.6	91249.3	127786.7	206117.3	375490.0	
Service Level 7:Public Kiosk							
Number of Accounts	545	795	1045	1165	1265	1365	
Consumption	895163	1587913	2370548	2958744	3576218	4274377	
Av. Consump. Per Account per Month	136.9	166.4	189.0	211.6	235.6	261.0	
Billing		317582.7	474109.6	591748.7	715243.6	854875.4	
Service Level 8:Utility water vending							
Number of Accounts	0	190	290	320	320	320	
Consumption	0	294841.6	486644.8	598350.1	676978.26	765938.76	
Av. Consump. Per Account per Month		129.3	139.8	155.8	176.3	199.5	
Billing		58968.3	97329.0	119670.0	135395.7	153187.8	
Service Level 9:Prepaid metered kiosk							
Number of Accounts	0	130	230	290	340	390	
Consumption	0	300785.9	569899.5	783430.5	1000715.3	1246324.6	
Av. Consump. Per Account per Month		192.8	206.5	225.1	245.3	266.3	
Billing		60157.2	113979.9	156686.1	200143.1	249264.9	
TOTAL DOMESTIC DEMAND	8028723	15586102	24941822	40895488	79232829	126236119	
NON-DOMESTIC DEMAND	16439877	20981912	26778828	34177324	43619889	55671260	
NON-DOMESTIC CONNECTIONS	8612	10991	14028	17904	22850	29163	
Commercial/Industrial	6465	8251	10531	13440	17154	21893	
Consumption upto 30m3/month.conn	775800	2970418	3791089	4838497	6175285	7881402	
Revenue from 1st step consumption	465480	2079292	2653763	3386948	4322700	5516982	
Revenue from 2nd step consumption	12531262	11502571	14680520	18736477	23913020	30519746	
Government/Institutional	2147	2740	3497	4463	5697	7271	
Revenue from Govt/Institutions	80847	4707774	6008445	7668468	9787124	12491126	
TOTAL NUMBER OF ACCOUNTS	37077	65226	96863	145159	255935	378748	
TOTAL REVENUE (million US$)	13.08	26.56	36.23	51.53	81.98	119.32	
TOTAL EXPENDITURE (million US$)	11.42	16.82	50.77	28.42	54.60	59.20	
Surplus/Deficit	1.66	9.74	-14.54	23.11	27.38	60.12	
Cumulated Surplus/Deficit	**1.66**	**34.55**	**30.73**	**85.42**	**44.95**	**283.54**	
TOTAL DEMAND (m3)	24468600	36568014	51720650	75072812	122852717	181907380	
Average Tariff (US$/m3)		0.73	0.70	0.69	0.67	0.66	
TARGET COVERAGE	31%	51%	62%	69%	87%	100%	
Year	0	5	10	15	20	25	

Annexe 2: Draft consumer survey format

WATER SECTOR SERVICE LEVELS AND COPING STRATEGIES IN INFORMAL SETTLEMENTS

To the Researcher: Please read the following statement to each consumer before you ask the questions.

My name is ……………………………and I am working for …………………………..on behalf of the Government of …..………. The Research Team is investigating how water supply organizations can provide and maintain improved water services for existing and potential customers.

We would like you to assist us by taking time to answer the following few questions. If you do not wish to answer a particular question please leave it out. You have been chosen to take part in the survey on a purely random basis. Your answers will be treated confidentially. Thank you for your co-operation

Survey location:……………………………………………………………..

What language is used for the interview?. ……….   Survey date ……………….

1. From where do you and other members of your household obtain water?

Please indicate all the water sources that are used by the people in your household and whether you use that water for drinking and cooking or other uses. Please also estimate the average number of 20-litre jerrycans that are collected each day from each source for your household (tick boxes as necessary).

	For drinking and cooking	Other uses	Average no. of jerrycans used a day from each source for your household
i) Your own piped water connection (inside your house)	☐	☐	………
ii) Your own piped water connection (outside your house)	☐	☐	………
iii) Buy water from your neighbour	☐	☐	………
iv) A shared yard water connection	☐	☐	………
v) Private vendor	☐	☐	………
vi) Water kiosk	☐	☐	………
vii) Public standpost	☐	☐	………
viii) Water tanker	☐	☐	………

	For drinking and Cooking	Other uses	Average no. of jerrycans used a day from each for your household
ix) Handcart /bicycle water vendor	▭	▭	....
x) Private open well	▭	▭	....
xi) Handpump	▭	▭	....
xii) Rainwater from roofs	▭	▭	....
xii) Spring water	▭	▭	....
xiii) From pools of water/lake or stream	▭	▭	....

Total   ....

(*Note – check where vendors obtain their water to avoid double counting)

2. What is the number of people in your household? ....

3. What is the average time to collect water for *all* the household *each day*? ....(minutes)

4. What is the distance to the nearest piped water source that you can use?....................................(metres)

5. What is the average price of water from local vendors? ....(per 20-litre jerrycan)

6. Average number of days per week that piped water is available? ....(answer if you use piped water)

7. What is the average number of hours of piped water per day?..............(answer if you use piped water)

8. Are you satisfied with the utility water services? (yes or no) ....(answer if you use piped water)

9. What is the average total household expenditure on water? ....(per week)

10. In you household, what percentage of water is collected by:

women: ....   children...........   men ....

11. How far from your house is there a functioning sanitation system such as a latrine or toilet that you regularly use?.......................................(metres)

12. What material are the walls of your house made from:

a) unburnt bricks............ b) burnt bricks or blocks .... c) mud and pole ....

Notes from the researchers after completing this form: (e.g. was the respondent able to answer the questions that are relevant for them, and any problems encountered or suggested changes?) To be included on a separate sheet.

www.ingramcontent.com/pod-product-compliance
Lightning Source LLC
Chambersburg PA
CBHW080952050426
42334CB00057B/2611